THIS BOOK IS PRESENTED TO:

_____

FROM:

_____

DATE:

_____

Copyright © 2021 by B&H Publishing Group
Nashville, Tennessee. All rights reserved.

978-1-0877-3012-7

Written by Aaron Armstrong
Illustrations by Heath McPherson, James Elston,
Benji Williams, David Miles, and Chloe Salvatore.
Copyright © 2021 by B&H Publishing Group

Dewey Decimal Classification: C220.95
Subject Heading: TRUTH / BIBLE. O.T. STORIES /
BIBLE. N.T. STORIES

All Scripture quotations are taken from the
Christian Standard Bible®, copyright © 2017 by
Holman Bible Publishers. Used by permission.
Christian Standard Bible® and CSB® are federally
registered trademarks of Holman Bible Publishers.

Printed in November 2020 in Dongguang, Guangdong, China
1 2 3 4 5 6 · 24 23 22 21 20

BIG TRUTHS
BIBLE STORYBOOK

written by
Aaron Armstrong

B&H
KIDS
Nashville, Tennessee

ONE BIG STORY

MANY BIG TRUTHS, ONE BIG GOD.

Think about some of your favorite people, like your best friend, a coach, a teacher, or maybe even your parents! Why are they your favorite? Is it what they teach you, the advice they give, or how they challenge you? While those things matter, I bet you love them not so much because of what they do and say but more because of who they are and how much they love you.

That's one of the big reasons we want to read the Bible. The Bible has so much to teach us about, well, *everything*. The Bible tells us the truth about the God who has always existed and what He is like. (**He is holy, loving, and good.**) It tells about how God made everything that exists—including us—and what He wants for His world and the people living in it. (**God made everything for His glory and our good.**) It teaches us why we see so much beauty and goodness, and also so much pain and sadness, in the world. (**God made the world good, but sin ruined everything.**)

The Bible teaches us all this and thousands more truths! But it doesn't tell us these things so we can just learn the facts. Behind all these big biblical truths stands the God who wants us to know Him as a person—to know what He is like, what He cares about, and how much He loves us. That's why God gave us the Bible as a story: one big story of His loving plan to save the world from sin by sending His Son, Jesus, to die on the cross, rise from the dead, and rule forever.

That's why this book exists too. We want to introduce you to the big truths of the Bible through the big story of the Bible so you can get to know our big God better. When you know what God is like, and when you understand how He has shown His love for you, it changes, well, *everything*.

OLD TESTAMENT

NEW TESTAMENT

1

GOD CREATED EVERYTHING

GENESIS 1:1–25

What's your favorite thing in the whole world? Maybe it's a book with an amazing story and beautiful illustrations. Maybe it's a toy you hold close at night. Maybe it's a pet you take care of and play with. Or maybe it's a special place, like a park or swimming pool.

Here's a better question: Why do we have favorite things? What makes them so great? Is it just that the thing itself makes us happy? Or do we sometimes love it so much because someone made it or gave it to us?

In case you weren't sure, there is Someone who made everything: God! But He isn't a person in the same way we are. He wasn't born. He doesn't grow or change. God doesn't even have a body, but He has always been here. God is alive, powerful, and amazing.

Once, long ago, when all that existed was God, He created the heavens and the earth. God took nothing, and He made everything from it.

Do you know how He did it? He spoke. For six days, God said, "Let there be . . ." and whatever He said, happened.

On the first day, light and darkness split, and day and night divided into time. On the second and third days, the sky and the earth separated, the sea and the land appeared, and plants sprang to life. On the fourth day, God created the sun and the moon. (He made the stars too!) On the fifth day, He made every creature that lives in the water and every bird that flies in the sky. On the sixth day, God made every kind of animal that lives on the earth—and even the ones that live in it too.

But why did God make all these amazing things? It wasn't as if He needed them. God doesn't need any of it—because He doesn't need anything! But God did have a reason, an important reason: He created everything for His glory. God made everything to show His amazingness—His creativity, power, love, and goodness.

If we were talking about someone else—*anyone* else—that would sound kind of self-centered. But not with God. He is the most amazing person that exists! He is the only One who should show off His awesomeness without hesitating. Because when He does, God is doing good. And He is doing so for our good so we can know Him, our good Creator.

God made everything to show His amazingness.

BIG TRUTH

God created everything for His glory and our good.

This means that everything exists to show us how amazing God is (His glory) and so we can enjoy Him (for our good). This is why food tastes good, why nature is filled with color, and why music exists. Creation helps us see what God is like and enjoy Him. The Bible says God's Son, Jesus, doesn't just show God's glory. Jesus is the glory of God. He perfectly shows the world what God is like, and through His death and resurrection, Jesus offers the greatest good imaginable: life with God forever.

BIG QUESTIONS

- What is your favorite thing in the world? What do you love most about it?

- What does your favorite thing tell you about God?

- How does your favorite thing help you enjoy God?

2

GOD'S FAVORITE CREATION

GENESIS 1:26–2:25

What do you think is the most amazing thing God made? Maybe you're thinking of something big and powerful, like a waterfall or a mountain range. Or maybe something small but whimsical comes to mind, like a snowflake or dandelion fluff. As great as these are, the Bible says God made something even more amazing—something more incredible than anything else in all the world. But what was it?

For six days, God made everything in creation—day and night, land and sea, plants and animals. And every time God made something, He said it was good. He loved it all. But God wasn't done. He still wanted to make one more thing, something that would be different from everything else. This creature would be made in God's image, care for the rest of God's creation, and live with Him as family.

God would make human beings—people like you and me.

When God made the first people, He didn't create them the way He did everything else. He didn't speak them into existence (although He could have done that). Instead, God formed the first man, Adam, from the dirt and breathed into him so that Adam came to life! But when God looked at Adam, He knew something was not good. It wasn't Adam himself that was the problem; God had made him exactly how He wanted.

The problem was that Adam was *alone.*

Adam needed someone else like him. He needed an equal to be his helper and his partner in everything. So God put Adam into a deep sleep and then made the first woman, Eve, from his side. When Adam awoke and saw her, do you know what he did?

He sang for joy!

Eve was wonderful; she was similar to Adam, but also different. Then God looked at these two, the man and woman, and He was glad. Together, they could show the world what God was like by enjoying the world and caring for it. Together, they could show each other what God was like by working, talking, learning, laughing, and cherishing one another. Together, the humans weren't just good, they were *very good.*

Together, they could show the world what God was like by enjoying the world and caring for it.

BIG TRUTH

God created everything for His glory and our good.

To be made for God's glory means that we can show the world what God is like through our attitudes, actions, and relationships. This is still true today, even though sin has broken our relationship with God and we often reject Him. The Bible says Jesus is the image of God who perfectly shows us what God is like. When we put our faith in Jesus, He repairs our relationship with God! Jesus helps us love God and show His character to others.

BIG QUESTIONS

- How does it make you feel to know you are different from the rest of God's creation?

- Name someone who shows you what God is like. How does this person reflect God to you?

- What is one thing you can do today to show someone what God is like?

3

EVERYTHING WENT WRONG

GENESIS 3

Did you know that everybody in the world has the same problem? We all think, say, and do things that we shouldn't. Sometimes it's by mistake; other times it's on purpose. And when that happens, it's called *sin*. Sin is a problem people have had for almost as long as there have been people.

After creating Adam, God placed him in a garden and told him he could eat from any tree in the garden except the tree of the knowledge of good and evil. Then God made Eve. Adam and Eve knew that if they ate the fruit from the one tree, they would die. Because Adam and Eve loved God, they wanted to obey Him.

Then a snake—or something that *looked* like one—came to Adam and Eve. It asked Eve, "Did God really say, 'You can't eat from *any* tree in the garden'?" Eve said the only forbidden tree was the tree of the knowledge of good and evil (which was true) and that they

weren't even allowed to touch it (which was not true).

"If we do, we will die," Eve said.

"You won't die," the snake lied. "God knows that if you eat it, you will be like Him."

So Eve began to wonder about God and His commands. After all, the fruit looked *really* good. Just looking at it brought joy. If eating it could make Eve wise like God, how could she not? Eve touched the fruit. She was still alive. Eve pulled it from the branch. She was still okay. She ate it and then gave some to Adam, who was right beside her. He ate it too. Then *everything* went wrong.

Adam and Eve didn't die immediately. But something *was* different. They had sinned and gone against God's commands. Because they sinned, they felt something new: shame. Adam and Eve realized they were naked and made clothes out of fig leaves. Then they heard God in the garden and tried to hide from Him! When God spoke to them, they blamed the snake and one another for what happened. Adam even tried to blame God.

God cursed Adam and Eve. Because they sinned, their lives would be filled with sadness, sickness, and broken relationships. And after all that, they would die, just as God had said. But God had made a promise for them—and a curse for the snake. God said that someday one of Eve's children would fight the snake. This man would be hurt, but He would destroy the snake. All the way back then, God was talking about Jesus.

Sin is a problem people have had for almost as long as there have been people.

BIG TRUTH

To sin is to think, say, or behave in any way that goes against God and His commands.

Ever since Adam and Eve sinned, all people sin. Your friends sin, your family sins, your teachers sin, and you sin! There is only one person who never sinned: Jesus Christ. Jesus perfectly obeyed God in everything He thought, said, and did—even by dying on the cross and rising again. When we believe in Jesus, God sees Jesus' obedience as ours, and Jesus gives us His Spirit to help us obey God's commands.

BIG QUESTIONS

- Imagine you were in the garden instead of Adam and Eve. Do you think you would have made the same choices they did?

- Do you think the consequences of sin are fair? Why or why not?

- In what parts of your life do you most need God's help to obey Him? Ask Him for that help today!

4

A FLOOD, AN ARK, AND A RESCUE

GENESIS 6–10

I'm sure you've realized by now that lots of people in the world make bad choices. Maybe you hear about it at home or on the news, or perhaps you see examples of it in your own life. It's easy to wonder why God doesn't do something. Why doesn't God just stop all the people who do bad things? Well, there was a time long ago when He did just that.

After Adam and Eve left the garden, life kept getting worse. Sin (thinking, saying, or behaving in any way that goes against God) spread from Adam and Eve to their children and then to their children's children. Sinning was all the people wanted to do. It got so bad that God was sorry He had made humans. They were His favorite creation, made in His image, made to reveal Him to the world. But all that was in their hearts was evil all the time! So God decided to cleanse the world of evil. He would send a flood, and it would destroy everyone.

Everyone, that is, except a man named Noah and his family.

Noah was not a perfect man, but he followed God. So God told Noah to build an *ark*, or massive boat, big enough for his family members and pairs of every kind of living creature—birds, livestock, and other land animals. Noah was a man of faith, so he did everything God commanded.

After all the animals and Noah's family were inside the ark, God shut the door. Then the rains fell and fell and fell. For forty days and forty nights, the rains did not stop—not until the entire surface of the world was covered. It was more than a year after the flood began until Noah, his family, and all the animals could finally leave the ark. When they did, Noah made an altar to worship God.

God was pleased with Noah's worship and sent a rainbow as a sign of the promise that He would never again flood the world. But the problem of sin still remained. Noah, like all people, would keep on sinning. The problem that began in the garden of Eden continued with Noah's descendants. To solve the problem of sin, God would have to do more than cleanse the world of bad people. He would need to send a Savior to cleanse people's hearts.

For forty days and forty nights, the rains did not stop.

BIG TRUTH

To sin is to think, say, or behave in any way that goes against God and His commands.

Sin is what we do naturally. Although some of us will never murder or steal, all of us will feel hate in our hearts or wish we had something someone else has. But God has been kind to us. He promised to never send a flood to cleanse the earth of evil people again. But more than that, God sent Jesus to die on the cross and rise again to pay for our sins. With Jesus, we have forgiveness from God, and we want to obey God and His commands most of all.

BIG QUESTIONS

- What is one problem you see in the world you wish God would make go away?

- We cannot fix our sin problem on our own. We need God to change our hearts. Do you believe that?

- What sin do you struggle with most right now? Take a moment and ask God to help you fight against that sin.

5

A PROMISE IS A PROMISE

GENESIS 12–21

Has anyone ever promised you something you had to wait for? It's not easy to wait on a promise—especially one that seems impossible. But Abraham and Sarah knew all about impossible promises. They also knew all about what happens when you try to make someone else's promise happen in your own timing.

For twenty-five years, Abraham held onto God's promise that he would have an *heir*, a son of his own, whose mother would be Sarah, his wife. God had said this heir would be the first of many descendants, as many people as the stars in the sky. (That's quite a large extended family!) Now, this sounded unlikely to Abraham and Sarah. When God made this promise—back when Abraham was still called "Abram"—they were already old and had no children. But God had changed Abram's name to "Abraham" as a reminder of the promise, one that God even repeated many times.

her husband to take her servant, Hagar, to be another wife to him, thinking this would be the way they could have a child.

Hagar had a son named Ishmael, but God told Abraham that Ishmael wasn't the promised child. God would keep His word through Sarah, just as He said. Nothing could stop God's good plan.

So Abraham and Sarah waited for twenty-five long years. Then when they were nearly one hundred years old, the miraculous happened. Sarah became pregnant. She had a son, a boy named Isaac. God brought Isaac into the world at just the right time. Abraham's family grew through Isaac, then through his son Jacob, and eventually, that led to Jesus. Jesus was a descendant of Abraham. Through faith in Jesus, millions and millions of people—as many as the stars in the sky—have become part of God's family.

God always keeps His word! For God, a promise is a promise, no matter what. He is in control of everything, and no matter what we see or experience, nothing is going to stop His good plans from happening.

Abraham believed that God was going to keep His word, despite his old age. But Sarah was another story. She desperately wanted a baby, and as far as she was concerned, that could never happen. She even laughed at the idea! Sarah was so full of doubt that she told

For God, a promise is a promise, no matter what.

BIG TRUTH

God is in control of everything in heaven and on earth. Nothing is outside of God's good plan.

No matter what we experience in life, we can hope in God's promises. God is in control of everything in heaven and on earth. Nothing catches God off guard, because nothing that happens is outside of His good plan. God's promise to Abraham began with the birth of Isaac, and that promise was fulfilled thousands of years later through Jesus. People from all nations are blessed through faith in Jesus when their sins are forgiven and they are welcomed into God's family!

BIG QUESTIONS

- Has someone ever broken a promise to you? What was it? How did you feel?

- Have you ever made a promise to someone else and then broken it? Why were you unable to keep it?

- What difference does it make knowing that God is in control of everything and never breaks His promises?

6

SIN CAN'T STOP GOD'S PLAN

GENESIS 37–50

Joseph seemed to have it all: He was the favorite of his father Jacob's twelve sons. He had a special coat made with many colors of fabric. He also had strange dreams—dreams where his brothers, and even Jacob, bowed down to him.

If Joseph seemed to have it all, his brothers seemed to be losing out. They were jealous of how their father treated Joseph, and they hated Joseph because of the dreams. Did Joseph really expect they would bow down to him? Not a chance! Filled with jealousy, they attacked Joseph, threw him into a pit, and sold him to a group of traders headed to Egypt. Then they told their father his favorite son was dead.

Joseph's brothers believed this was the end of Joseph's dreams. But they (and Joseph) didn't know that these dreams were part of God's plan for their family. By selling Joseph

into slavery, his brothers were making sure the dreams eventually came true!

In Egypt, Joseph became a trusted servant to Potiphar. But when Potiphar's wife lied about Joseph, he was sent to prison. In prison, Joseph met the king's cupbearer and interpreted a dream for him. Joseph asked the cupbearer to tell the king about him. The man promised he would. Unfortunately, he forgot.

Joseph suggested that the king store extra grain so they would have enough food during the famine. The king agreed, and he put Joseph in charge of the project.

The famine came, and people from all over went to Egypt to buy grain from Joseph—including his brothers. They didn't recognize him at first, but they did bow down to him. When Joseph revealed his identity, they were terrified! They expected Joseph to take revenge, but instead Joseph forgave them. He told them that even though they meant to harm him, God used their evil actions for good.

Two years later, the king began having strange dreams himself. The cupbearer remembered Joseph and told the king that he could interpret them! With God's help, Joseph explained that the dreams were a warning: Egypt would have seven years of great harvests followed by a seven-year-long famine when food would be scarce.

God brought Joseph—and eventually, his entire family—to Egypt to save them from harm. They stayed in Egypt for many years, but Egypt wasn't their true home. God had a place in mind for them. And just as God brought His people into Egypt, he would bring their descendants out again.

BIG TRUTH

God is in control of everything in heaven and on earth. Nothing is outside of God's good plan.

We may not understand everything that happens to us, but God has a good plan for this world, and for us. God is in control of everything in heaven and on earth, which means that He uses everything—even the sinful choices of people—to make sure His plan happens. God used Joseph's brothers' wicked actions to save many people from harm, including the brothers themselves! Thousands of years later, God would use the sinful choices of people who put Jesus on the cross to offer a way for all people to be saved from sin.

BIG QUESTIONS

- Have you ever felt jealous of someone else? What made you feel that way?

- How do you think Joseph felt when he was sold by his brothers and then put in jail? How did you think Joseph felt after he realized what God was doing?

- Are there hard things happening in your life right now? How does Joseph's story change how you think about them?

7

GOD SENDS A RESCUER

EXODUS 1–4

Moses was afraid. But let's be honest: you would be afraid too if you heard your name being called out from a bush. Especially if that bush were on fire. And even more so if the flames weren't burning.

But it wasn't just hearing his name from a bush that scared Moses. It was what the voice asked him to do: go to Egypt and tell the Pharaoh, Egypt's king, to let the Israelites go free.

The Israelites were the descendants of Jacob's family. They had lived in Egypt for many years. For a long time, they were treated with kindness because of all the good Joseph had done for Egypt. But eventually a king came along who did not remember Joseph. When he looked at the Israelites, he only saw a threat to Egypt. There were so many of them. What if they sided with an enemy during a battle? Egypt would be ruined! So this king treated the Israelites cruelly. He made them slaves and forced them to build Egypt's cities.

But God was with the Israelites. He had promised their ancestors years before that He would make their family great and that all nations would be blessed through them. Even though the Israelites were being treated cruelly in Egypt, they would not stay there. Just as God had brought them to Egypt, He would bring them out of it.

Moses knew all this. After all, he was an Israelite. But he also grew up as part of the king's family. He saw how badly the Israelites were treated. He even tried to stop it, but he failed. That's why he was in a distant land, tending sheep.

Then the voice came out of the burning bush—*God's* voice.

"Moses, I am sending you to Egypt," God said. "You will tell the king to let My people go!"

But Moses was afraid. He made all kinds of excuses:

"I stutter."

"The people won't believe me."

"Can't someone else go?"

"No, you are going," God said. "I will tell you what to say. You will perform wonders in My name, and your brother, Aaron, will go with you too. The king of Egypt will let My people go."

Moses returned to Egypt. When he found the people, he told them everything God had said. They praised God because He was going to keep His promise to rescue them.

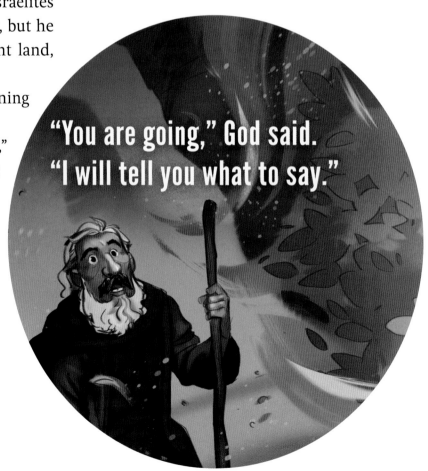
"You are going," God said. "I will tell you what to say."

BIG TRUTH

God always keeps His promises because He is faithful.

To be *faithful* means to be steady, constant, and trustworthy. Moses' anxiety and fear couldn't stop God's faithfulness. The king of Egypt's power couldn't stop His faithfulness. Later, the Israelites' doubt and unbelief couldn't stop God's faithfulness. Because of God's goodness, power, and faithfulness, we can trust Him with our whole lives and obey Him in every situation. Even when we are afraid or unsure, and even when we cannot see the future, we can know God will keep His promises and we can walk in obedience.

BIG QUESTIONS

- Why do you think Moses kept making excuses instead of obeying God? If you had a stutter, would you want to talk to a king?

- Have you ever felt afraid to do something God's Word says to do? What was it?

- Why is it a good reminder for you right now that God always keeps His promises?

8

THE EXODUS

EXODUS 5–15

Moses' first meeting with the king of Egypt didn't go the way he hoped. Moses and Aaron went to the king as God commanded, even though Moses was afraid. They asked for the Israelites to be set free. *Maybe this won't be difficult,* they thought. *Maybe the king will do what God wants.*

But he didn't.

The king refused to let the Israelites go. He wasn't going to listen to Moses and Aaron, or to their God. Even when Moses and Aaron revealed God's miraculous power by turning Aaron's staff into a snake, he wouldn't change his mind. Moses warned the king that God would judge Egypt if he didn't release the Israelites, but he ignored the warning flat out.

So Moses and Aaron left, and that's when the plagues began.

First, God turned all the water in Egypt into blood—all the lakes, rivers, and ponds. The entire country smelled horrible, but the king still wouldn't set the Israelites free.

Next, God sent frogs into Egypt, then gnats, and then swarms of flies. After that, the Egyptians' livestock died, and the people suffered from painful sores. Next, God sent hail that ruined the Egyptians' crops and locusts that ate the rest. Eventually, God sent darkness that covered the whole land.

Every time God sent a plague, the king promised to release the Israelites. But then he thought about it more and changed his mind. He broke his promise every time.

Finally, Moses warned that if the king did not let the Israelites go, the firstborn male in every family would die. But death would pass over every home with the blood of a spotless lamb spread on its doorposts. In faith, the Israelites followed Moses' instructions. This night would eventually be called *Passover* because death "passed over" the Israelites' homes.

Sadly, the king *still* didn't listen to God. At midnight, the final plague came, and the king's firstborn son died along with many others. After that, the king finally said the Israelites could leave. They walked out of Egypt and toward the Red Sea. But soon, the king regretted his decision, and he sent his army after them!

When the Israelites saw this, they were afraid. But Moses reminded them that God is faithful. Then he raised his hand over the sea, the waters parted, and the Israelites walked across on dry land. When they were on the other side, the waters crashed back down onto the Egyptian army.

God's people were finally free!

God's people were finally free!

BIG TRUTH

God always keeps His promises because He is faithful.

Sometimes it's hard for us to believe in God's faithfulness when He doesn't do things how we expect Him to. Whether it's Moses, Aaron, and the Israelites waiting through ten plagues before leaving Egypt, or Jesus' body lying in a tomb for three days before He came back to life, God is always faithful to keep His promises! Because God is faithful, we can trust Him with everything that's going on, no matter what.

BIG QUESTIONS

- How do you think the Israelites felt when they were finally freed from Egypt?

- How does it feel when something you've been waiting for finally happens?

- What are you waiting for right now? How do those examples help you trust God today?

41

9

RULES TO LOVE GOD BY

EXODUS 19–20

Worship is a strange word, isn't it? What does it make you think of? Lots of people think of worship as singing songs. While singing is certainly part of it, *worship* is about celebrating the greatness of God. That means worship is a part of everything we say and do.

The Israelites didn't understand this quite yet, but they were about to. They had spent three months wandering in the wilderness after leaving Egypt. Every day, God provided for their needs in miraculous ways. He made a special food called manna fall to the ground every morning. He provided water for the people when none could be found. He even gave them quail at night after they complained about missing meat. God was so kind to the Israelites. Soon they arrived at the place where He was leading them: a mountain called Sinai.

Thunder and lightning filled the sky. Smoke covered the mountain. The people were afraid. God's presence was on the mountain, and it was terrifying! But God called

Moses up Mount Sinai to speak with Him. Through the smoke, thunder, and lightning, Moses climbed. There, God gave him a set of commandments, or rules for how the Israelites were to live and worship God as His people:

1. There is one God, so only worship Him.

2. Don't worship other gods or make images or statues to worship.

3. Don't misuse God's name in any way.

4. Set one day per week apart as a special day to rest and worship God.

5. Honor your parents.

6. Do not murder people.

7. Keep your marriage vows.

8. Do not steal.

9. Do not lie about others.

10. Do not be jealous for things that aren't yours.

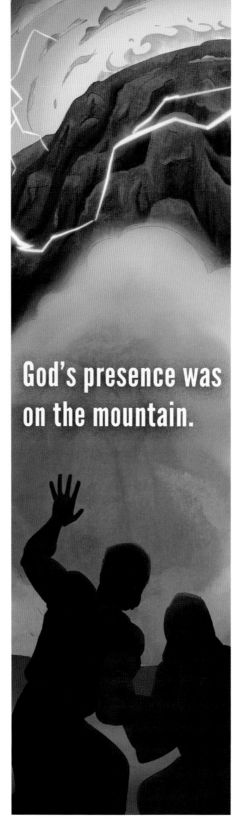

God's presence was on the mountain.

These commandments were rules for living—but they weren't *just* rules. The point of them was to show the people how to worship God and celebrate His greatness. God wanted His people to see that worshipping Him involved every part of their lives.

When Moses descended the mountain, he shared the Ten Commandments with the Israelites. Upon hearing them, they promised to keep God's rules and worship God with everything. But God knew they would never be able to keep all Ten Commandments perfectly. He knew that His people had a problem greater than captivity in Egypt. Their hearts were still set on sin. But someday He would free them from that too!

BIG TRUTH

Worship is celebrating the greatness of God.

God commands us to worship Him with our whole lives because He knows it's the best thing for us. For example, God knows that lying harms our hearts, while honoring our parents brings wisdom. Worship is celebrating the greatness of God. It means showing the world who God is, what He is like, and what He is doing. Keep in mind that God does many great things, but the greatest thing He ever did was send Jesus! When we believe in Jesus, we will want to worship God and for others to see how great God is.

BIG QUESTIONS

- What is your favorite way to worship God?

- Think about a rule that's good for you that you really don't enjoy doing (like cleaning your room). How can that be an opportunity to worship God?

- Which of the Ten Commandments is hardest for you to follow? Do you want God's help? Ask Him!

10

MOSES' FRUSTRATION AND FOOLISHNESS

NUMBERS 13–14, 20

Everyone gets frustrated sometimes, even with people they care about. Frustration can make us forget what people are truly like. And when our frustration overwhelms us, we can make foolish mistakes.

Moses was frustrated. He and the Israelites had traveled for months, walking from Egypt to Sinai and then to Canaan, which was the land God promised would be their home. The people were grumbling and complaining most of that time about almost everything.

When they came near to Canaan, Moses sent twelve spies in to see what the land was like. When they returned, they brought back pomegranates, figs, and grapes. The fruit of the land was amazing, but ten of the spies warned everyone against going in. "The people who live there are too strong," they said. "Their cities have solid walls." They doubted God and asked, "Why has God led us all this

way when we clearly cannot conquer this land?" So the people refused to even try. They didn't believe God could lead them to defeat their strong opponents.

This frustrated Moses, and it angered God. God declared that this group of people—the people He had rescued from Egypt—would not enter the Promised Land. They would have to wander for forty years. Then they would die in the wilderness.

Months passed in the desert. Moses's frustration grew. The people were complaining again, about water this time. Because God loved them, God told Moses to speak to the rock and call water out from it. But when Moses looked at the people, his anger poured over. Instead of speaking to the rock, Moses grabbed his staff and struck it.

Water gushed from the rock, and the people drank! But God was not pleased with Moses. He knew that when Moses struck the rock, he was really striking at God. He knew Moses was angry, not just with the people but with Him.

In that moment, Moses had forgotten what God is like. He had forgotten that God had been with him throughout all the ups and downs of leadership. He had also forgotten that God is holy, good, and loving. Moses sinned and failed to demonstrate God's character to the people as their leader.

Because of his sin, God told Moses he could not enter the Promised Land either. But God did not abandon Moses or His people. Even when they failed to honor Him, God continued to demonstrate what He is like—holy, good, and loving.

When our frustration overwhelms us, we can make foolish mistakes.

BIG TRUTH

God is holy, good, and loving.

Sometimes we can forget what God is like, especially when frustrating, hard, or bad things happen. That's why we always need to remember that God is holy, good, and loving. God is morally perfect, everything He does is for our good, and He loves us. Sometimes it might not seem like this is true, but that's because we cannot see the bigger picture; we cannot understand what God is doing behind the scenes. When we start to lose faith like the Israelites and Moses did, we can look to Jesus. He gave us the perfect picture of God's holiness, goodness, and love when He died on the cross and rose again.

BIG QUESTIONS

- Do you think Moses was right to be angry with the Israelites? How about angry with God?

- What was the most recent thing you got angry about? Why did it upset you? How did you react?

- Do you ever forget that God is holy, good, and loving? What might help you remember this truth?

11

GOD'S GOOD NEWS FOR JOSHUA

JOSHUA 1

Do you know God speaks to us? God made the world in a way that tells us what He is like; it shows us how amazing and powerful He is! But God doesn't just want us to know that He exists. He wants us to know Him—and He wants us to know ourselves. That's why He gave us His messages in the Bible.

After Moses died in the wilderness, God spoke to a man named Joshua. Joshua had been Moses' assistant for many years. He loved God and wanted to obey Him. God told Joshua that he would lead the Israelites into the Promised Land, and this would be a difficult job. The land was filled with strong enemies, and the Israelites did not have a powerful army. But God promised never to abandon Joshua or His people.

"I am with you. I will not leave you," God said. "Be strong and courageous."

"I am with you. I will not leave you," God said. "Be strong and courageous."

This was good news for Joshua! Their armies would not have to try to take the land in their own power. God would be with them in defeating their enemies—in fact, God was going to be the One who defeated them!

In addition to leading the people into the Promised Land, Joshua would also guide them to trust the commandments God had given to Moses. God told Joshua to treasure His words deep down in his heart. He said, "This book of instruction must not depart from your mouth; you are to meditate on it day and night" (Joshua 1:8). God knew that if Joshua did this, every decision he made as a leader would reflect wisdom, understanding, and godliness. But trusting God's commands that much would take courage.

It would take faith and strength not to back down when others wanted to rebel.

So Joshua told the people to get ready. He said, "We will enter the Promised Land, the land where God will give us rest." The Israelites promised Joshua they would do everything they were commanded. And they encouraged Joshua, just as God had, to be strong and courageous because God was with him.

What God told Joshua way back then is what God still tells His people today. He says, "I am with you. I will never leave you." God has given us His Word, and He wants us to treasure it deep down in our hearts, just like Joshua and the Israelites did.

BIG TRUTH

The Bible is God's Word that tells us what is true about God and about ourselves.

The most important book in the whole world is the Bible. The Bible is God's Word that tells us what is true about God and about ourselves. Studying the Bible shows us why God made us and what He commands us. With the Holy Spirit's help, God's Word leads us, strengthens us, and makes us courageous to live for God. Most important, the Bible reveals God loves us so much that He sent His Son Jesus to die on the cross for our sins and rise from the dead. Now, like Joshua, we don't have to fear anything!

BIG QUESTIONS

- Why do you think God wants us to know Him?

- What is a question you've had about God for a while? Spend some time with a grown-up to see if you can find the answer to your question in the Bible.

- Have you tried to memorize a Bible verse, hiding it deep down in your heart? If not, John 3:16 is a great place to start. If you've already memorized that one, what other verse might you try?

12

GOD'S POWER OVER JERICHO

JOSHUA 2, 6

Have you ever seen a miracle? Well, miracles don't happen every day (if they did, they wouldn't be miracles), so maybe you haven't. But that doesn't mean that miracles aren't real. Miracles are special, supernatural events that could not happen on their own, and miracles always have a purpose.

When God's people entered the Promised Land, they were told to go to the city of Jericho. It had very strong, tall walls that no army could easily break through. Tearing them down would take a miracle! But God was at work.

Joshua sent two spies into Jericho to see what they were up against. It wasn't long before the guards learned they were there, so the spies found a place to hide with a woman named Rahab. She told them that everyone in Jericho was afraid of the Israelites because they knew God was going to defeat their city

Rahab asked the spies to make a promise: "Will you spare my family when you defeat Jericho?" The spies agreed to this but told her to give them a sign. Rahab put a scarlet cord in the window so they would know which house to spare.

Later, when the Israelites approached the city of Jericho, God told them not to attack. Instead, they were to march around the walls of the city once a day, for six days. On the seventh day, they marched seven times with the priests blowing ram's horn trumpets. On the seventh time around the city, the priests blew their trumpets as loud as they could, and the Israelites all gave a loud shout.

Then the walls of Jericho collapsed. It was a miracle!

This miracle, like every miracle, had an important purpose: it revealed to everyone watching that God is far more powerful than men. In fact, He is all-powerful. The walls of Jericho were strong and mighty, but they could not stand against God's strength. What God promised would happen, happened. The spies also kept their promise to Rahab and spared her and her family.

The battle of Jericho was only the beginning of the Israelites' journey in the Promised Land. There were more battles to fight, and the Israelites would win them. God would perform many more miracles in the process. God had promised to give the land to His people—and nothing could stop Him from fulfilling His word.

Then the walls of Jericho collapsed. It was a miracle!

BIG TRUTH

A miracle is something God does that usually cannot be done so that we can know He is all-powerful.

The Bible is full of miracles. A *miracle* is something God does that usually cannot be done so that we can know He is all-powerful. When the walls of Jericho collapsed simply because of some shouts and horns, that was a miracle! In the New Testament, when Jesus fed the large crowd with one lunch and healed people no doctor could help, those were miracles. Every miracle in the Bible had a purpose. God's greatest miracle happened when Jesus rose from the grave. Jesus is alive today, and everyone who trusts in Him will have all of their sins forgiven. That's a miracle too!

BIG QUESTIONS

- Why does God do miracles?

- How does Rahab's request for her family to be spared show that she had faith in God?

- How do you think the Israelites felt when the walls of Jericho fell?

13

THE SELFISH JUDGE OF ISRAEL

JUDGES 13–16

Have you ever been given a warning? Chances are, you have. Everyone has moments when they are warned not to do something (even grown-ups!). But we don't always listen to warnings, do we? Sometimes we just want to do what we want to do. Sometimes we are selfish.

Kind of like Samson.

Samson lived during the time when judges led the community of Israel. At the time, God's people did what they wanted to do—sinning and worshipping false gods instead of the true God. God used people groups like the Philistines to punish the Israelites, but God also sent judges to rescue them.

Before Samson was born, God told his parents that when Samson grew up, he would lead the Israelites. He told them to make a vow, dedicating their son to God; and as a sign of that vow, Samson was never to cut his hair.

As Samson grew up, he became very strong—stronger than any normal person—but he was also selfish and arrogant. He married a Philistine woman, even though the Philistines didn't follow God. Again, Samson wanted what he wanted, even if it wasn't best. When he and his wife had a fight, he stormed off. Assuming that Samson had ended their marriage, his father-in-law allowed his daughter to marry someone else. So, Samson set the Philistines' fields on fire and, using the strength God had given him, killed a thousand men using a bone as his only weapon!

Then Samson married another Philistine woman named Delilah. The Philistine leaders told Delilah to find out the secret of Samson's strength so they could capture him. After tricking her twice, Samson told her the truth: if his hair was cut, he would lose all his power. So, when Samson went to sleep, Delilah cut off all his hair. The Philistines took Samson away in chains, beat him, and brought him to the temple of their god.

Humbled because of what had happened, Samson asked God to give him strength one more time so he could destroy the Philistines. Samson put his hands on the pillars of the temple, and he felt God's power flow through him. He pushed as hard as he could, and the pillars broke! The entire temple collapsed, killing everyone inside—including Samson.

The Israelites saw what happened to the Philistines and Samson, but sadly, they didn't change. Yet God continued warning the people against sin because His warnings were for their good.

Samson wanted what he wanted, even if it wasn't best.

BIG TRUTH

The fair payment for sin is death.

People today are just as selfish and arrogant as Samson and the Israelites were. God gives us commands that are for our good, but we often ignore Him and do what we want to do. In other words, we sin. Even though the fair payment for sin is death, God is kind to us. He warns us about sin's payment, and He sent Jesus to take on our punishment when He died on the cross and rose from the dead. When we trust in Jesus, the Holy Spirit helps us think about what God wants and not just what we want. He helps us heed God's warnings and follow Him. He helps us be less selfish and more humble.

BIG QUESTIONS

- Have you ever been warned against doing something and then did it anyway? What happened?

- Do you think warnings are a good thing or a bad thing? Why?

- What should we do when we are tempted to ignore warnings, either from God's Word or from wise people around us?

14

GOD'S SOMETIMES-HARD-TO-SEE GOODNESS

THE BOOK OF RUTH

We all face times when we think we're being treated unfairly. Sometimes we even think God is treating us unfairly! But thinking something is true doesn't make it true. This is what a woman named Naomi had to learn.

Naomi had moved to a country called Moab because there wasn't enough food in Israel. There, she and her family had all they needed. Her sons got married. Life was good. Then suddenly, her husband and her sons died, and Naomi was left alone with only her daughters-in-law, Orpah and Ruth.

Why did this happen? Was God punishing her? Naomi didn't know, but her heart was sad and bitter. She thought God was treating her unfairly. Then she told Orpah and Ruth to go back to their own families, while she would return to Israel. Ruth did not agree to this. She promised to stay with her mother-in-law, no matter what.

In Israel, Naomi's bitterness continued. Then one day something incredible happened. After gathering grain on the edges of the field, her daughter-in-law, Ruth, returned home excited. She had met a man named Boaz, the owner of the field she worked in. He treated her kindly and sent extra grain home with her!

Hope began to break through Naomi's bitterness. Would God finally bring some good out of her suffering? After all, Boaz was a relative of her husband. He was a *family redeemer*—someone who could protect her and Ruth—in this case, by marrying Ruth and purchasing Naomi's husband's land.

Naomi encouraged Ruth to go and speak to Boaz, and when Ruth did, Boaz agreed to marry her. But first they had to talk to someone else: another possible family redeemer. Boaz asked the man if he would buy Naomi's land and marry Ruth. The man took off his sandal, gave it to Boaz, and said, "You do it." This was a way that Israelites agreed to make exchanges at the time.

So Boaz married Ruth, and they had a baby named Obed. All the people celebrated, even Naomi. She could finally see how God had brought good out of her difficult situation.

But that wasn't the end of the good God was doing. Obed grew up and had a son named Jesse, who had a son named David, who became Israel's king. Then, hundreds of years later, from David's family came Jesus, the redeemer of the whole world.

Naomi could finally see how God had brought good out of her difficult situation.

BIG TRUTH

The fair payment for sin is death.

The Bible says that the fair payment for sin is death, but that doesn't always mean people die because of a sin they personally commit. Like what happened in Naomi's family, sometimes people die because sin brought suffering and death into the world, and now death is a part of our lives. When we face hard times in life, we need to remember that suffering, sadness, and death won't last forever. God has promised to make the world new! Hard experiences in our lives help us look forward to the day when everything sad—even death—will be gone forever.

BIG QUESTIONS

- Have you ever felt like God is treating you unfairly? Why?

- Have you ever seen something good come from something terrible? What happened?

- How does God's care for Naomi and Ruth encourage you?

15

ISRAEL'S FOOLISH FIRST KING

1 SAMUEL 11, 13

What we say and do matters. For example, have you noticed that when you speak and act kindly, your relationships get stronger? But what happens when you do hurtful things? Relationships can be ruined that way.

King Saul should have remembered this.

Saul was Israel's first earthly king. When God chose him to take the throne, Saul was surprised because he wasn't anyone special. But when Samuel the priest poured oil on him and prayed, God's Spirit came upon Saul. Then, God gave Saul power and victory over their enemies, the Ammonites. Because of the victory, the people trusted Saul as their king. They rallied behind him. But Samuel the priest warned the people and Saul: "If you worship and obey God, God will be with you. But if you disobey Him, God will be against you."

Saul had been crowned king when he was thirty years old, and he ruled for forty-two years, fighting many battles. For a long time, Saul obeyed and worshipped God, and God was with him, just as Samuel had said. But when he became older, he made a foolish choice that ruined everything.

After Saul's son, Jonathan, attacked the Philistines—an old and powerful enemy of the Israelites—three thousand Israelite troops came together at a city called Gilgal. The Philistines also gathered their troops—so many that they couldn't be counted—at a place called Michmash. The Israelites were afraid of the size and strength of the Philistine army. Some hid in caves. Others cowered across the Jordan River. But Saul waited. He knew he could only win if God was with him. Samuel the priest had promised he would come to worship God and make a sacrifice before the battle, but Samuel was running late. So Saul made a foolish choice.

"Bring *me* the burnt offering and the fellowship offerings," he said.

Saul made the sacrifices instead of waiting for Samuel. Doing so went directly against God's commands. Kings weren't allowed to make sacrifices—only priests like Samuel could.

When Samuel arrived, he asked, "What have you done?" Saul said he was sure the Philistines were going to attack, and there was no time to wait.

"You have been foolish," Samuel said. "Because you disobeyed God, your kingdom will be taken from you."

Then Samuel left, and Saul went with him. The Philistines attacked, and Israel lost the battle. Saul's foolish words and actions broke his relationship with God. He was still king, but not for long.

What we say and do matters.

BIG TRUTH

Because God is holy, sin has broken our relationship with God.

God is *holy*; He is pure and perfect in every way. Because God is holy, sin has broken our relationship with God. There is nothing we can do on our own to fix the mess we make of things with our foolish choices. But God sent Jesus into the world to do what we cannot: restore our relationship with God. By living a perfect life, dying on the cross, and rising from the grave, Jesus offered us what we could never earn for ourselves: a restored relationship with God. When we trust in Jesus, every foolish choice we ever make is forgiven.

BIG QUESTIONS

- Have you ever done something foolish? What happened?

- Imagine you were Saul and you were waiting for Samuel to arrive while your enemies closed in. Do you think you would have done anything different? Why?

- Why do you think we can't fix our relationship with God on our own? Why is Jesus the only One who can?

16

GOD'S GRACE TO ISRAEL

1 SAMUEL 16-18

Has someone ever given you something you knew you didn't deserve? Maybe it was one of your parents doing something really kind for you after you had disobeyed them. Do you know what that's called? It's called grace. *Grace* is when we receive something good even when we don't deserve it. No one is as gracious as God.

When King Saul went against God's commands, his sin ruined their relationship. Samuel no longer came to speak to him, God's Spirit left him, and God chose someone else to be king. But even though Saul had sinned, God was still kind to him. Samuel didn't see Saul again, but he still prayed for him. The kingdom wasn't going to be his forever, but Saul was still king. God's Spirit left him and he was troubled by evil spirits, but listening to the music of the shepherd boy named David made Saul feel calm.

Then God showed great kindness to Israel when they faced the Philistines and their great champion, Goliath. Goliath was a giant and a skilled warrior for the Philistines. The Israelite army was terrified of him. Even Saul was afraid! What could they do against a mighty enemy like this?

Soon, David the shepherd boy arrived on the battlefield. He went to Saul and said he would fight Goliath. Saul wondered how David could defeat a giant who had been a warrior since he was a child. After all, David wasn't even a fully grown man. But David said, "God protected me when I fought the lions and bears to protect my sheep. If God can do that, He can help me defeat Goliath."

So David faced Goliath with only his sling and a handful of stones. The giant saw David approach and began to mock him. But David said, "You have defied the Lord, and He will hand you over to me!"

The giant laughed. David ran, took a stone, and slung it at Goliath—hitting him square in the forehead. The giant stopped laughing. He fell to the ground. The Philistines turned and ran, and Israel's army fought against them.

After his victory, David became part of Saul's court and army. He even married Saul's daughter. The Israelites loved David, and they saw that God was with him. Saul did too.

God showed great kindness to Israel when they faced the Philistines and their great champion, Goliath.

BIG TRUTH

Grace is when God gives us something good even when we do not deserve it.

Because of his sin, Saul didn't deserve God's help against the Philistines, but God sent David as a gift of grace. Because of our sin, we don't deserve all the good things God gives us either. But God is kind. He gives us breath in our lungs and creation to enjoy. He gives us friends and family. He gives us wisdom to make hard decisions. And most important, God gave us Jesus to defeat our greatest enemies—sin and death! Because of Jesus, we can love God and live with Him forever.

BIG QUESTIONS

- How would you describe *grace* in your own words? Have you ever experienced grace?

- Why does God do good things for people who don't deserve it? Why is Jesus' sacrifice on the cross the greatest sign of God's grace?

- Who is someone in your life you could show grace to?

17

GOD'S COVENANT WITH KING DAVID

2 SAMUEL 6–7

Even though David was just a boy when God promised he would be king, he didn't officially become king until he was thirty years old. During those in-between years, King Saul knew that God was with David and saw that the people loved him. So Saul became jealous and tried to kill David to keep him from being king! But David trusted God and refused to treat Saul the way Saul treated him, showing him respect and kindness instead. When Saul died, David ruled over the kingdom faithfully. But ruling faithfully didn't mean he ruled perfectly.

As king, David was charged with protecting the ark of the covenant, a symbol of God's presence with His people. The ark was kept in the home of a man named Abinadab, and David wanted to bring it back to Jerusalem. Even though God's Law said that only the priests could carry the ark using gold-covered

poles, David put it on a cart instead and began the journey home.

On the way, the oxen pulling the cart stumbled and the cart tipped. A man named Uzzah caught the ark and died. David was afraid! He wanted to do a good thing for God, but he didn't do it the way God commanded. Three months later, he brought the ark back to

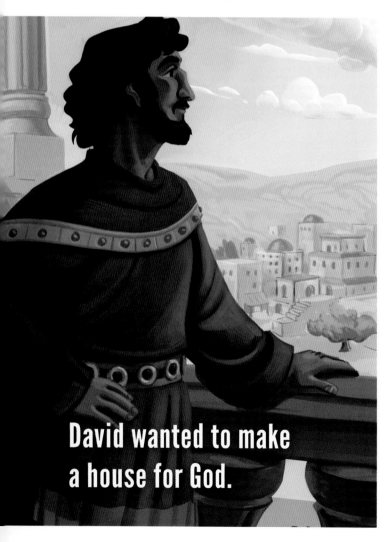

David wanted to make a house for God.

Jerusalem—this time the way God wanted—and all the people sang and danced for joy.

A while later, David looked at his home, which was made of wood, and compared it to the tent where the ark was kept. David wanted to make a house for God—a temple where people from all over the world could come to worship Him.

God sent the prophet Nathan to speak to David. "God says, 'You wanted to build Me a house, but I haven't asked for one. Instead, I am going to make a *covenant* with you, David.' (A *covenant* is another word for a commitment, or a promise.) 'One of your descendants will build a house for Me. I will make His kingdom last forever. I will be a father to Him, and he will be My Son. My love will never leave Him or you!'" God was talking about the *Messiah*, or rescuer, who would save His people not from their physical enemies but from their deeper problem: their sins.

David thanked God for His grace. David knew that he and the people didn't deserve this promise, but he also believed that God would keep it. David was right: even when David's descendants rebelled against Him, God didn't reject them.

BIG TRUTH

Grace is when God gives us something good even when we do not deserve it.

Throughout David's life, God showed him grace, giving him good things when he didn't deserve them. Even though he loved God, David was a sinner like everyone else. He didn't always do what God commanded. Yet God was gracious to David. He made a covenant, or promise, that one of David's descendants would be king forever. God fulfilled that promise when Jesus came into the world as a member of David's family. Jesus is God's greatest sign of His grace. He is our gracious King, and His Kingdom will never end.

BIG QUESTIONS

- David was a faithful king, but he was also a sinner. Why do you think the Bible wants us to know this about David?

- David wanted to build a house for God, but God had something better in mind. Why do you think God's covenant to David is important for us today?

- Do you believe God ever stops loving His people?

18

GOD'S GIFTS TO KING SOLOMON

1 KINGS 2-3

If you could ask for anything, what would it be? Most of us would probably ask for things like money, fame, or power. But do you know what's better than that? Wisdom.

When King David was an old man, he chose his son Solomon to be the next king. Solomon was young but wise, and he knew that there would be many problems he would encounter as king. One of those problems was dealing with his father's enemies. One of those was a man named Shimei.

Shimei had spoken cruelly and cursed David many years before. David showed mercy on him and promised not to punish him in the way he deserved. But before he died, David told Solomon he would need to deal with this man.

Solomon told Shimei to build a house in Jerusalem and live there. As long as he stayed there and did not leave, he would face no punishment for his treatment of David. But if he ever left, he would receive the punishment he deserved.

Solomon showed mercy to Shimei, and for three years, Shimei lived peacefully. But one day, Shimei learned that two of his servants had run away. Even though Solomon said to never leave his home, Shimei went after them and brought them back. When Solomon heard, he sent his guards to find Shimei, and Shimei was punished just as Solomon had said he'd be.

Even though Solomon was already wise, he knew he needed more wisdom to be the kind of king Israel needed. One night after he worshipped God, God spoke to Solomon.

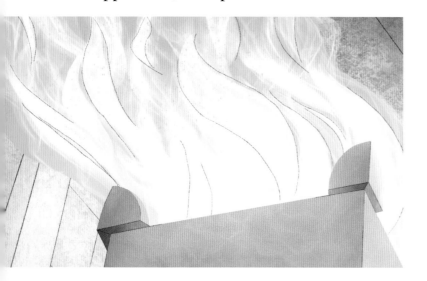

"Ask anything you wish, and I will give it to you," God said.

There was only one thing that Solomon wanted. "I am young and inexperienced," Solomon said. "Please give me the wisdom to judge faithfully and know the difference between good and evil, so that I can rule your people well."

Solomon's answer pleased God, and God gave him what he asked for. In fact, God did more than just give Solomon wisdom. He gave him all that the king did *not* ask for: wealth, power, and long life if he obeyed God like David did.

For many years, Solomon ruled wisely and obeyed God faithfully. But when he became old, Solomon sinned. He treated his people cruelly, worshipped false gods, and foolishly disobeyed God's commands. In His mercy, God didn't take the kingdom away from Solomon. He continued to love him, just as He promised David He would.

One night after he worshipped God, God spoke to Solomon.

BIG TRUTH

Mercy is when God does not give us the punishment that we deserve.

Solomon was merciful to Shimei for many years, giving him a way to avoid the punishment he deserved. When Solomon behaved foolishly in his later years, God had mercy on him by not punishing him for worshipping false gods. God had mercy on us by sending His Son Jesus to take on the punishment we deserve! Because of God's great mercy toward us, we have the ability to show mercy to others.

BIG QUESTIONS

- Why do you think Solomon asked God for wisdom?

- Has anyone ever showed you mercy? What did you do, and how did they respond?

- God wants us to show mercy to others just like He shows mercy to us. Who in your life needs to receive mercy?

19

PRAYING FOR GOD'S MERCY

1 KINGS 6–9

When Solomon was king of Israel, people came from all over the world to hear from him. He was very wise—wiser than any king before or after. He wrote many songs and even more wise sayings. But Solomon knew it wasn't enough for people to hear his wisdom. God gave Solomon the job of building a temple where people could come worship Him.

The temple was very large and beautiful. Gold and bronze were everywhere! It was exactly the kind of place you'd expect someone as holy and magnificent as God to be worshipped.

When the temple was finished, the Israelites celebrated. The priests offered sacrifices to *dedicate* it, or set it apart, for God. Solomon asked God to bless the temple. He prayed that people from all over the world would come to the temple, see how amazing God is, and worship Him too.

Then Solomon prayed for God to show the people *mercy*, or to not punish the people as their sins deserved. He understood that all people sin in big and small ways. He knew the Israelites would fail to obey God's commands, so he prayed that God would listen to anyone who asked Him to forgive them. He also asked for protection when they rebelled and were captured by their enemies. Over and over, Solomon prayed for God to show the Israelites mercy.

When the celebration was over, God spoke to Solomon again, promising to hear the people's prayers and show them mercy. But He also warned that if the Israelites or Solomon turned against Him and worshipped false gods, they would experience the consequences of that sin.

While it might not seem like it, this is the most loving thing God could have said. To remove all consequences of sin is not loving at all. Sin is too serious to treat that way. This is why God promised to show the people mercy, but He would not ignore their sins entirely.

Solomon loved God, but he also loved other things. While he was king, he had many wives, which went against God's command about marriage. His many wives worshipped false gods, and eventually Solomon did too.

God showed Solomon and his family mercy, but Solomon still had to face the consequences of his own sins. His kingdom would be taken away, but not while Solomon was alive, and not all of the kingdom. Again, this was a sign of God's mercy.

God promised to show the people mercy, but He would not ignore their sins entirely.

BIG TRUTH

Mercy is when God does not give us the punishment that we deserve.

God does not ignore people's sins, but He does show people mercy. Mercy is when God does not give us the punishment that we deserve. God is merciful to us because He warns us about what will happen when we sin—our lives are harder and the consequences are real. God is also merciful to us because He promises to forgive our sins through Jesus. Because of what Jesus has done, we can ask God to forgive every big or small sin we ever commit. Every single time, God will forgive us. Sin does not stand between us and God anymore. Our God is a God of great mercy!

BIG QUESTIONS

- How would you explain God's mercy in your own words to someone who has never heard of it?

- Why is it important for us, as Christians, to understand God's mercy?

- Do you ever feel like God won't forgive you when you sin? Take some time to read and remember Hebrews 4:16 and 1 John 1:9.

20

GOD DEFEATS THE IDOLS

1 KINGS 16–18

After Solomon died, Israel was divided into two kingdoms. Solomon's descendants ruled the southern kingdom called *Judah*. The northern kingdom, *Israel*, had many different kings. Both kingdoms had one thing in common: they all went against the one true God and worshipped false gods, or *idols*.

The worst of the northern kings was King Ahab. Ahab made a temple for an idol named Baal and set up places to worship other idols all through Israel. After this, God sent a *prophet*, or messenger, named Elijah to warn Ahab. Elijah said that God would punish Israel for worshipping false gods like Baal. Because the people rebelled against Him, there wouldn't be enough food in the land, and it wouldn't rain again until Elijah said it would.

Three years later, Elijah and King Ahab met again. Ahab blamed Elijah for the famine in Israel. But Elijah reminded Ahab that there

The people needed God to do a miracle inside their hearts.

But Baal didn't answer. No fire came from anywhere.

Then Elijah prepared his sacrifice. After it was ready, he poured large jugs of water all over it. He poured water on the wood a second time, then a third. Then Elijah prayed. "LORD, you are God in Israel. Answer so their hearts will turn back to you!"

Suddenly, fire came down from heaven. Everything was burned up—even the water Elijah had poured over the sacrifice. The people were amazed and worshipped God. Soon, a rainstorm arrived and the downpour started. The drought was over! The Lord had proven that He was the one true God.

Even though the people worshipped God in that moment at Mount Carmel, their worship didn't last. It wasn't enough for them to see a miracle. It wasn't enough for God to send rain. The people's hearts were set on sin. They loved their idols more than they loved God. To change for good, they needed more than to watch a miracle with their eyes; they needed God to do a miracle inside their hearts.

wasn't enough food or water because he had disobeyed God's commands and worshipped idols. Then Elijah told the king there would be a test to decide who was the true God: the Lord or Baal. Baal's priests and Elijah would each offer a sacrifice at Mount Carmel, and the god who sent fire from heaven would be declared the one true God.

Everyone gathered at Mount Carmel. Baal's priests prepared their sacrifice. They prayed, danced, and shouted as loud as they could. They even started hurting themselves.

BIG TRUTH

Idolatry is a sin of the heart in which we love and value something else above God.

Because of sin, we don't want to love God the way He deserves. Instead, we commit idolatry. *Idolatry* is a sin of the heart in which we love and value something else above God. We can do this with anything in our lives like money, food, toys, school, sports, or even other people. When we trust in Jesus, God's Spirit changes our hearts and gives us the power to love Him above everything else. Because of Jesus, we can enjoy every good thing God gives us *and* still love God most of all.

BIG QUESTIONS

- What do you think it would have been like to see fire come down from heaven? What would it have shown you about God?

- Why do you think the people who saw the miracle at Mount Carmel returned to their former ways after a while?

- What is one idol that you think you might be worshipping right now? Will you admit that to God and ask Him to change your heart?

21

A (TEMPORARY) RETURN TO WORSHIP

2 KINGS 12; 2 CHRONICLES 24

While the kings of the northern kingdom of Israel only worshipped false gods, thankfully, some of the kings of the southern kingdom of Judah led the people back to God.

Joash was one of those kings. He was raised by the high priest, Jehoiada, and became king of Judah when he was only seven years old. Soon after becoming king, Joash commanded that the temple be repaired. The priests were to use the silver they were given to restore any damages they found.

But for twenty-three years, no work was done! So Joash commanded that the priests not take any more silver for themselves. Instead, whenever the offering chest was full, it was emptied and given to Joash. Then he and Jehoiada gave the silver to workmen who hired stonecutters, carpenters, blacksmiths, and coppersmiths to restore the temple.

The people carefully worked to rebuild the temple, and when they finished, they returned the remaining gold and silver so that new articles for the temple could be fashioned. For the rest of Jehoiada's life, Joash and the people worshipped God in the temple and gave their offerings and sacrifices to Him.

Unfortunately, this didn't last. They eventually began worshipping idols again. After Jehoiada died, even Joash turned away from God. So God sent other prophets to speak with the king, but he wouldn't listen. He wouldn't repent, or turn away from his sin, and neither would the people. After Joash died, some kings of Judah called the people back to God, but others led them astray.

Restoring the temple was important, but it wasn't enough. It wasn't enough to provide a temple for worship if the people's hearts were far from God. It wasn't enough to teach the words of God in the temple if the people refused to hear them. The people needed to repent—to truly turn away from sin— but to do that, they needed something else.

They needed new hearts to understand the truth. The temple building wasn't what mattered; the God who dwelled there, the God who could change their hearts—He is who mattered most.

It wasn't enough to provide a temple for worship if the people's hearts were far from God.

BIG TRUTH

Repentance is turning away from sin and turning to Jesus.

During the reign of every one of Israel and Judah's kings, God called the people to repent. *Repentance* is turning away from sin and turning to Jesus. When we repent, we are sorry for our sin. We also communicate with our thoughts, words, and actions that God is more valuable to us than anything else. The first thing Jesus said when He started preaching was, "Repent!" This is how important repentance is to living a life of faith. Repentance is the starting place for following God, and it's something we continue to do every day as Christians.

BIG QUESTIONS

- **What do you think it would have been like to be king at just seven years old?**

- **Why do you think restoring the temple wasn't enough to keep people focused on God?**

- **How would you describe repentance in your own words?**

22

SALVATION FOR ALL PEOPLE

THE BOOK OF JONAH

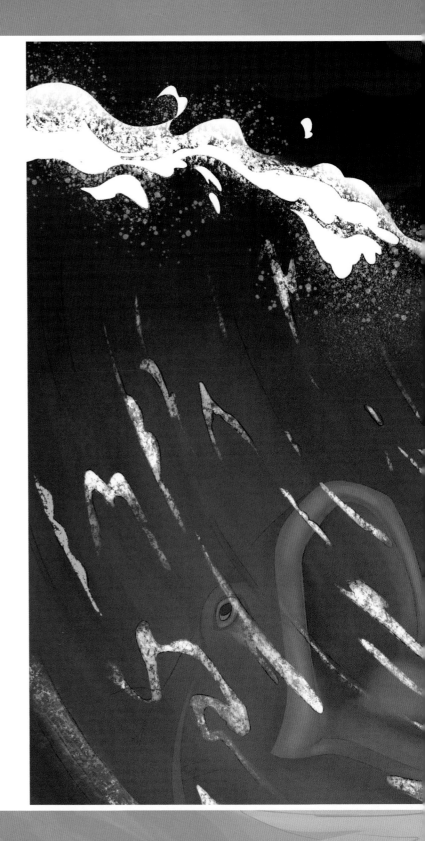

For a long time, God sent prophets to Israel and Judah to remind them of how much He loved them. But God made it clear that He cared about other people groups too. After all, He had saved Rahab, Ruth, and others who had not descended from Abraham. Sadly, His people ignored this fact. Some even thought that they were the only people God *should* love.

So when God told the prophet Jonah to go to the people of Nineveh, Jonah was angry. The Ninevites were evil and cruel. As far as Jonah was concerned, they *deserved* God's judgment.

So Jonah left and boarded a boat for Tarshish, which was the exact opposite direction of Nineveh. While they sailed, God sent a storm that nearly caused the boat to sink. When Jonah told the other sailors that the storm had come because he was running away from God, they were terrified.

They threw Jonah overboard and asked God to forgive them. As soon as Jonah hit the water, the storm stopped, and a giant fish appeared and swallowed Jonah whole.

In the belly of the fish, Jonah remained alive. He prayed, thanking God for His mercy. Even though Jonah didn't deserve it, God had saved him from death. After three days, the fish spit Jonah onto dry land. This time, when God told Jonah to go to Nineveh, he went. When he arrived, he warned of God's judgment, "In forty days, Nineveh will be demolished!"

The people believed him. They fasted and prayed. Everyone, including the king of Nineveh, called out to God, asking for forgiveness. God heard their cries and did not destroy the city. God showed compassion to the Ninevites, which is exactly what Jonah figured would happen. And he didn't like it.

So Jonah left the city and made a shelter, waiting to see if God might destroy the Ninevites anyway. While he waited, God made a plant grow and give Jonah shade, which made Jonah happy. Then the next day, God sent a worm to eat the plant, and it withered up. Jonah was angry at this—so angry he asked God to let him die.

But God said to him, "Is it right for you to be angry? You care about this plant. Why can't I care about these people (the Ninevites), who do not know right from wrong?"

Jonah had no answer for God. God's point was clear: All people are special to God, and He will have compassion on anyone He chooses.

All people are special to God, and He will have compassion on anyone He chooses.

BIG TRUTH

People are special because we are made in God's image, as male and female, to know Him.

God shows His love to all people in many ways. The Bible says God makes the rain fall and the sun shine on both the good and the evil (Matthew 5:45). God also sent His Son, Jesus, into the world to save all kinds of people. We may think that certain people are so bad they don't deserve God's love. But that is not for us to decide. God shows compassion to whomever He chooses. This is why God tells us to go out into the world and tell everyone about Jesus.

BIG QUESTIONS

- Why do you think God spared Jonah's life? Why do you think Jonah still got angry with God at the end of the story?

- All people are made in God's image—even the people we don't like. How does this change how you think about people?

- How might you show kindness to someone who doesn't know Jesus?

23

GOD'S JUDGMENT OF JERUSALEM

2 CHRONICLES 36

How many times have you been warned to look both ways before you cross the street, but there have been no cars? Or how many times have you been warned not to run at the pool, but you see someone else run, and they don't fall? Sometimes warnings seem pointless. We hear one, and we're tempted to ignore it because the danger doesn't seem real. But all it takes is one car or one wet spot, and we're in a life-or-death situation.

For hundreds of years, after David and Solomon ruled as kings of Israel, God's people went against Him. They disobeyed His commands and worshipped false gods. God warned them over and over again through the prophets about what would happen if they continued to sin. But the people ignored every warning. They even laughed at the prophets. Although God had always been right before, they didn't listen or trust in His words now.

Finally, God was done with giving warnings. He had been patient with His people, showing them mercy. But He could not ignore their sin any longer.

So when Jehoiakim was king of Judah, Nebuchadnezzar and the Babylonians attacked Jerusalem. They captured Jehoiakim and took him to Babylon in chains, which meant his son Jehoiachin became king.

Three months and ten days later, Jehoiachin was taken away to Babylon too. His brother Zedekiah was made king. Zedekiah was proud and did not listen to Jeremiah, the prophet God had sent to speak to him. When Zedekiah refused to swear loyalty to either Nebuchadnezzar (the king of Babylon) or to God, Nebuchadnezzar destroyed Jerusalem.

In Jerusalem, the Babylonians took everything valuable from the temple and burned it. They tore down the wall that surrounded the city. They burned the palaces and took every precious item. The people were chained and taken away, forced to serve Nebuchadnezzar and his successors.

The people felt hopeless. They had come to the Promised Land hundreds of years before, after God had freed them from captivity in Egypt. Now they were right back where they started: captives and servants in another kingdom.

But even as His people were led away from Judah, God wasn't finished with them yet. They were special to Him, and He had a plan for them. God would use Judah's captivity to prepare their hearts for their eventual return home.

God could not ignore their sin any longer.

BIG TRUTH

People are special because we are made in God's image, as male and female, to know Him.

When God sent the people of Judah into captivity, it wasn't because He didn't love them. It was because He wanted them to see how bad sin really was. This is still true today: God wants us to heed His warnings and do what He says is best for us, the ones He made in His image. Like God's people, when we sin, we will often face the consequences of that sin. But we won't receive the full punishment our sins deserve because Jesus took that when He died on the cross.

BIG QUESTIONS

- When you hear the same warning many times without anything happening, do you have a hard time believing the warning? Why?

- Imagine you were one of the people taken captive and sent to Babylon. What do you think you would have thought about along the way?

- How do God's warnings in the Bible show us that He cares about us? Why is it important that we pay attention to them?

24

THE WRITING ON THE WALL

DANIEL 5

When they arrived in Babylon, God's people probably wondered if God had abandoned them completely. After all, they had failed to live faithfully, and as punishment, they were now in *exile*, or an extended time away from their homeland. But God had promised long ago that He would never leave His people. No matter where they were—in the Promised Land or in exile—God was always with them and always loved them.

A teenager named Daniel understood this. As a captive in Babylon, he was put in the service of King Nebuchadnezzar. There, he faced many temptations to compromise his faith. He was given a new Babylonian name and offered rich foods that went against the Israelites' diet. But Daniel did not forget where he was from: he ate only water and vegetables and kept his faith in God. God blessed him for this, and Daniel became a powerful advisor to Nebuchadnezzar for many years.

Because of Belshazzar's pride, God had judged him.

More than sixty years after God's people were brought to Babylon, a new king, Belshazzar, ruled. He was foolish and proud, and one night during a great feast, Belshazzar used one of the cups stolen from God's temple to drink from.

Suddenly, a hand appeared in the air and wrote a message on the wall. Belshazzar didn't understand the message. He called for the wise men in the palace, promising them power and wealth if they told him what the writing meant. But none of them could understand it. Then, the queen said, "There is a man who can interpret this message. His name is Daniel. He used to serve Nebuchadnezzar and was chief of his wise men. The spirit of the gods lives in him. Send for him, and he will tell you its meaning."

So King Belshazzar called for Daniel, making the same promise of power and wealth he made to the other wise men. Daniel was not interested in Belshazzar's offer. But he did tell the king what the words meant: Because of Belshazzar's pride, God had judged him. That very night, the kingdom of Babylon was going to fall to the Medes, a more powerful empire.

Everything happened exactly as Daniel said.

When Babylon fell and the Medes ruled in their place, God remained with Daniel and His people. The exile would eventually come to an end after seventy years, and God would bring His people home.

BIG TRUTH

God is in all places at all times and is always with His people.

Daniel trusted God even while in exile in Babylon. He understood that God is in all places at all times and stays with His people. Hundreds of years after this story took place, God sent His Son, Jesus, into the world to live among us. Jesus no longer walks among us on earth, but the Holy Spirit lives in the hearts of everyone who trusts in Jesus. No matter what circumstances we face or how alone we might feel, we can remember that God is everywhere; He is always with us.

BIG QUESTIONS

- Is it sometimes hard to believe that God is in all places at all times?

- How does it make you feel to know that God never leaves His people, no matter how bad circumstances might get?

- Take some time to read and memorize God's promise from Deuteronomy 31:6. Why is remembering this promise important to you today?

25

OUT OF EXILE

EZRA 1-3

Living in exile, or away from their homeland, was difficult for God's people. While some, like Daniel, became powerful members of the king's court, most lived ordinary lives in Babylon. But no matter where they lived or what they were doing, all God's people were waiting to see if God would keep His promise.

God had told His people that after seventy years, they would be free to return home. While they waited, they built homes, raised children, and had jobs. During that time, they saw Nebuchadnezzar die. They saw Belshazzar's kingdom rise then fall. Now Cyrus the Persian ruled over them. They wondered, *Will Cyrus let us go? Will God keep His promise?*

Within the first year of his reign, the people had their answer. Cyrus wrote a *decree*, or an order that must be obeyed. The order said that any of the Lord's people who wanted were free to return to Jerusalem and rebuild the temple. Not only that, but Cyrus ordered

that people in every region of his kingdom provide silver, gold, goods, livestock, and even special offerings to be taken to their temple.

Why on earth did Cyrus do this? There was no reason for him to allow these people—people he was holding captive—to return to their homeland. It must have seemed crazy to everyone who heard Cyrus's decree. But Cyrus wasn't crazy. He let the people go because God led him to do it. God had promised the exile would end, and God's word can always be trusted.

Some people were happy to stay in Babylon, but more than forty thousand people chose to return to Jerusalem. Cyrus also sent with them all the gold and silver basins, knives, bowls, and other items Nebuchadnezzar had taken from their temple.

When the people finally arrived in Jerusalem, there was a lot of work to be done. But before they started on their tasks, they did the most important thing they could, something they hadn't been able to do for seventy years. They worshipped and offered sacrifices to God! As they rebuilt the temple, and then later, the walls of the city, God continued to be with them.

More than forty thousand people chose to return to Jerusalem.

BIG TRUTH

God cannot lie or ever be wrong, so we can trust whatever He has said.

Everything God says He will do, He will do! God said His people would be in captivity in Babylon, and it happened. He said they would be freed after seventy years, and it happened. Throughout the Bible, God promised to send Someone to save us, and Jesus came. God promised that Jesus would die and rise from the dead, and He did. Because God never lies and is never wrong, we can live with faith, hope, and joy. We can trust God!

BIG QUESTIONS

- How do you think those forty thousand people felt while returning from exile to Jerusalem?

- Why do you think they worshipped God before getting to work on rebuilding the temple?

- Because God is trustworthy, He wants us to be trustworthy too. Have you told someone you would do something, but you haven't followed through? If you can, take a minute now and do it.

26

GOD GIVES ESTHER COURAGE

THE BOOK OF ESTHER

Fifty-eight years had passed since Cyrus released God's people from exile. In that time, they lived mostly peaceful lives throughout the Persian empire. But it only took one man to put their lives in danger once more.

That man was Haman, who should have been the happiest man in Susa. King Ahasuerus promoted him, giving him the most important position in the kingdom. Everyone bowed down to him. Everyone, that is, except a man named Mordecai.

Haman was furious. Didn't Mordecai know he was a really big deal? Haman tried to find out what was going on and learned that Mordecai was a *Jew*, which was another name given to God's people because they were from the land of Judah.

Haman could have talked to Mordecai or simply let it go. But he was too proud. Instead, he planned to have all the Jewish people in

the entire kingdom killed, and he made an evil plan to trick the king into signing the order.

Unfortunately, Haman didn't know that the queen, Esther, was Jewish. But Mordecai knew because he had raised Esther as his daughter. So when Mordecai learned of Haman's plans, he told Esther about it. Esther asked him and all the Jews in Susa to pray and fast for her for three days.

Three days later, Esther went to the king, uninvited, which meant she could get in a lot of trouble. But King Ahasuerus welcomed her. "Ask for anything, up to half my kingdom, and it will be done," he said. Esther invited him and Haman to join her for a feast. Haman was thrilled—even the queen knew how important he was! At the banquet, King Ahasuerus asked Esther again what he could do for her.

Queen Esther courageously saved her people.

"My people and I are in danger," she said. "Someone is planning to kill us." The king was very upset hearing Esther's news. "Who could do something like this?" he said. "This evil man is Haman!" she said. The king was outraged. Haman begged for his life, but the king took him away and executed him.

It was too late to take back the king's original order, so King Ahasuerus sent out new orders, allowing the Jews to defend themselves. Soon, the threat was over. The Jewish people survived, and every year from then on the Jews held a celebration remembering how Queen Esther courageously saved her people.

BIG TRUTH

When we sin, we should feel sorry that we have disobeyed God and want to turn from our sin because we love Him.

Haman sinned in many ways. He was proud and thought he was more important than others. He planned evil things against the Jewish people, and he even lied to the king to make it happen. When Haman was found out, he wasn't sorry for his sin. He only wanted to avoid being punished for it. When we are caught sinning, we often feel like Haman. But this isn't what God asks of us. When we sin, we should feel sorry that we have disobeyed God and want to turn from our sin because we love Him.

BIG QUESTIONS

- Have you ever believed or acted like you were more important than another person? Why do you think God calls that sinful?

- Why can we always confess our sins to God—no matter how big they get?

- Esther risked her life to save her people from Haman's evil plan. In a similar way, the Bible encourages us to put others first and care about what happens to them. How can you do this today?

27

THE PEOPLE'S PROBLEM RETURNS

EZRA 7–10; NEHEMIAH 8

When Ezra the priest left Babylon for Jerusalem, he had high hopes for God's people. He knew that Israel was sent into captivity because they had broken God's commands. Now that they were free once more, he wanted to teach them to carefully obey God so they would not repeat their parents' and grandparents' mistakes.

When Ezra arrived in Jerusalem, he offered sacrifices to God for the sins of the people. Then the Israelites' leaders came to Ezra to share troubling news: Many of the men had married women who worshipped the same kinds of false gods that drew Israel away from God hundreds of years before. And these weren't just any men; the people's leaders and the priests were the culprits. The people who were supposed to lead the Israelites to follow God were leading them to be unfaithful instead.

The people needed Someone to put God's Law in their hearts.

Ezra was devastated. With his face toward the ground and weeping, Ezra prayed. "LORD, forgive us; we have abandoned Your commands! After all that has happened to us because of our sins, should we do the same things again?"

As Ezra prayed, an extremely large group of men, women, and children gathered around him. They began to cry as well, asking God to forgive them. They promised to live according to God's Law. For a while they did, but it didn't last.

Later, when a man named Nehemiah became the governor, the people asked Ezra to teach the Law again. Ezra read from the scrolls for hours, with priests translating for him since not everyone could speak the Hebrew language. As he taught, the people realized they had *again* turned away from God's commands. They cried and prayed for God to forgive them.

Sadly, this repentance didn't last.

The Israelites faced the same problem after their exile that they had faced before it. They tried to obey what Ezra taught, but despite their best efforts, they were tempted to do what they wanted, what they felt like doing, and to ignore God.

Ultimately, the people needed Someone to do more than teach them God's Law like Ezra. They needed Someone to put His Law in their hearts. They needed the *Messiah*, or the rescuer God had promised would come through King David's family.

BIG TRUTH

When we sin, we should feel sorry that we have disobeyed God and want to turn from our sin because we love Him.

Loving God is what makes us want to turn from sin. Knowing what's in the Bible is good, but it's not enough. Memorizing Scripture is helpful, but it doesn't save. And trying to obey God in our own power simply doesn't work. We need the Holy Spirit to change our hearts, empower us to understand God's Law, and point us back to Him. The Holy Spirit leads us to love and obey God far more than we ever could on our own.

BIG QUESTIONS

- How do you think Ezra felt when he saw the Israelites continue to sin?

- Why is knowing God's Law important, but not enough?

- What is something you know you shouldn't do, but you keep doing it? Have you asked for forgiveness? Have you asked God for help to change that?

28

THE LAMB OF GOD APPEARS

MATTHEW 1:18–25; LUKE 2:1–20; JOHN 1

It had been hundreds of years since God's people had returned to the Promised Land. The temple was restored. The walls of Jerusalem were rebuilt. But the people weren't free. The Roman Empire now reigned over the land, and no one from King David's family ruled. The people were watching and waiting for the Messiah, the rescuer God had promised long ago.

They knew the signs the prophets had spoken about: the Messiah would be born in Bethlehem. He would be a part of David's family. He would be called *Immanuel*, which meant "God with us." He would suffer for the sins of the people. Despite all this, they didn't know *when* He would arrive.

One day, an angel appeared to a man named Joseph from a town called Nazareth. Joseph was a descendant of King David. (But he wasn't a king.) He was supposed to marry a young woman named Mary, but there was a problem. Mary was going to have a baby. She explained that the baby was from the Holy Spirit. Joseph loved her, but this news was confusing to him, and he wasn't sure what he should do. The angel told Joseph that Mary was telling the truth. "Marry her, and name the child Jesus, because He will save His people from their sins."

Joseph did just as the angel said. Later, he went with Mary to Bethlehem to be counted in a census. When the time came for Mary to have the baby Jesus, she was staying in a place where animals were kept. She even laid Him in an animal feeding trough to sleep.

Soon, a group of shepherds came to them. They said an angel had appeared in the sky, declaring that "Messiah, the Lord" had been born. Mary thought deeply about what was happening. Her son was God's Messiah!

As He grew up, Jesus was a kid like any other in many ways. He ate, slept, played, and learned. But there was something different about Jesus. Unlike every other person, including His parents, Jesus never sinned. Most people did not understand who Jesus was, but they would soon find out.

When Jesus was a grown man, a prophet named John the Baptist saw Jesus walking by. He told everyone who could hear the good news: "There He is! The Lamb of God who takes away the sins of the world!"

Mary's son was God's Messiah!

BIG TRUTH

Jesus lived a sinless life, died on the cross, and rose from the dead.

In the Old Testament, people sacrificed a lamb as payment for their sins. The lamb took the person's place, and the person was not punished. When John called Jesus "the Lamb of God," he was telling everyone that Jesus had come to sacrifice His life to take our place. Jesus would save people from their sins! Because Jesus is God, He lived a sinless life, died on the cross, and rose from the dead. Jesus is alive today, and everyone who believes in Him is forgiven forever.

BIG QUESTIONS

- How do you think Mary and Joseph felt when the shepherds called Jesus the Messiah? Do you think they were excited? Scared? Nervous? Worshipful?

- Is it hard for you to believe that Jesus never sinned (not even once)?

- People at this time in history understood what sacrifices were for. What do you think the crowd thought when they heard John call Jesus "the Lamb of God"?

29

BAPTIZING THE MESSIAH

MATTHEW 3; MARK 1:1-11

Before Jesus began His ministry, a man named John spoke to the people. John was not like everyone else. He lived in the wilderness, dressed in a camel-hair coat, wore a leather belt around his waist, and ate locusts and wild honey. But John had an important job—one the prophets had spoken about many years before: he would prepare the people for the Messiah.

John told the people to *repent*, or to turn away from sin. "Get ready—the Lord is coming!" he said. "The one coming after me is more powerful than I am. I am not even worthy to untie His sandals. So get ready!"

People from all over the land listened to John. They confessed their sin against God, and John *baptized* them. This meant he dipped them under the water of the Jordan River and brought them up again as a sign of their repentance and desire to live a new life.

When Jesus came out of the water, something amazing and unexpected happened.

One day, Jesus came to John to be baptized. John was very confused.

"You want me to baptize You?" he asked, appalled. John knew that Jesus was sinless, so He did not need to repent or live a different life. "But I should be baptized *by* You!" John said.

"Trust Me," Jesus said. "I know you don't understand it, but this is the right thing to do."

So John baptized Jesus in the Jordan River. When Jesus came out of the water, something amazing and unexpected happened. The Holy Spirit came down looking like a dove and rested on Jesus. Then a loud voice called out from the sky, "This is my beloved Son; I am very pleased with Him." God the Father was speaking to the people about Jesus, from heaven.

After all of this, John's ministry was fulfilled. Jesus was the promised Messiah! He was the one John had been preparing the way for, and Jesus would do far more than just call the people away from sin. He would *save* people from the power of it. John baptized people with water, but baptism is a one-time thing. Jesus would die for people and then send the Holy Spirit to dwell in their hearts so their lives would be changed forever.

BIG TRUTH

Jesus lived a sinless life, died on the cross, and rose from the dead.

Jesus wasn't baptized because He had any sin of His own. Jesus never sinned! Instead, He was baptized because it was God's plan. Through His baptism, Jesus showed the world that He would die for our sin and rise again, offering new life to all who follow Him. God the Father knew that Jesus would suffer for sin and told everyone that day that He was pleased with Jesus. Jesus lived a sinless life, died on the cross, and rose from the dead. Jesus is the One the people had needed for so long!

BIG QUESTIONS

- Why did John the Baptist say Jesus was more powerful and important than he was? How did we see this play out in this story?

- How do you think you would have responded to the Spirit coming down like a dove and the Father speaking in a loud voice from heaven?

- If any of your family members believe in Jesus, ask them if they have been baptized. What was it like? Why did they do it? Do you want to be baptized one day?

30

LIVING WATER FOR A SAMARITAN WOMAN

JOHN 4:1-42

After Jesus was baptized, lots of people began to follow Him and became His *disciples*. Being a disciple was kind of like being His student. Jesus' disciples followed Him wherever He went, learned from Him, and helped Him in His ministry.

From the very beginning, Jesus did things that didn't make sense to His disciples. He taught hard-to-understand truths about God. He also made strange choices like going to Samaria (a place almost every Jew avoided) on their journey to Galilee.

It had been a long trip, and Jesus was tired, so He sat down at a well while His disciples went into town to find food. Soon, a Samaritan woman came to draw water, and Jesus asked her for a drink. The woman was surprised. Jesus was a Jew; she was a Samaritan. Jews and Samaritans didn't talk to one another.

But Jesus told her that if she knew who she was talking to, she would ask Him for a drink, and He would give her *living water*. He explained that anyone who drinks living water will never be thirsty again.

The woman was confused. Jesus didn't even have a bucket! And what did He mean by living water? In fact, Jesus wasn't talking about literal water. He was referring to eternal life with God.

The woman and Jesus kept talking, and soon she realized there was something different about Jesus. She asked Jesus questions about where people ought to worship God. Jesus told her that the particular place didn't matter; it was about worshipping in Spirit and in truth.

Then she said, "I know that the Messiah is coming. He's going to explain all this."

"I am the Messiah," Jesus replied.

The woman was so amazed, she ran off and told the townspeople to come meet Jesus. At the same time, the disciples arrived and asked Jesus what was happening. Jesus told them this was why they had come to Samaria: many Samaritans were ready to turn from their sins and follow God.

The disciples didn't understand. From everything they were taught, the Messiah was supposed to be for the *Jewish* people. As the disciples continued to follow Jesus, eventually they would see: God didn't send the Messiah just for one group of people. Jesus had come to forgive the sins of everyone in the world who would believe in Him!

Jesus explained that anyone who drinks living water will never be thirsty again.

BIG TRUTH

We can know that God loves us because He gave us Jesus to forgive the sins of the world.

The Jews of Jesus' day thought that salvation only belonged to them and that people like the Samaritans especially didn't deserve it. But God's love was not meant to stay with only one group of people. From the beginning, God had been rescuing all kinds of people, and He would continue to do so. We can know that God loves us because He gave us Jesus to forgive the sins of the world. Everyone, from any place and any background, can come to God and be made right with Him by believing in Jesus.

BIG QUESTIONS

- Knowing that Jews and Samaritans were enemies, how do you think the Samaritan woman felt when Jesus talked to her?

- What do you think it means to worship God "in Spirit and truth"?

- Who is someone in your life who needs to know about Jesus and how much God loves them?

31

JESUS, THE AMAZING AND POWERFUL TEACHER

LUKE 4:31-44

Jesus and His disciples traveled to many different towns to tell people the good news: "The kingdom of heaven is near!" they said. Jesus taught in *synagogues*, or places of worship and learning, in homes, and in public spaces too. Wherever He went, Jesus told people about what it meant to be part of God's kingdom. And sometimes, when He taught, incredible things happened.

In a town called Capernaum, the people were amazed by the things Jesus said. "He's not like the other teachers," they said. "He teaches with authority." But one day, as Jesus taught, a man started shouting. This man had an evil spirit in him.

"Leave us alone!" the man yelled. "Have you come to destroy us? I know who you are, Jesus; you are the Holy One of God!"

Imagine standing in the room and hearing this. You would probably wonder, *Why is this man calling Jesus the Holy One of God? Is He saying that Jesus is the Messiah—the rescuer God promised us?* Before you could ask your questions, Jesus spoke to the spirit.

"Be quiet," Jesus said. "Come out of that man!" Suddenly the evil spirit was gone, and the man was acting normal again. He was healed! Everyone who saw what happened was astonished. *Who is Jesus, and why would spirits like that obey Him?* they wondered. The people began to talk about what they saw, and soon, the word about Jesus began to spread throughout the region.

Who is Jesus, and why would spirits like that obey Him?

Jesus performed other miracles like healing the sick and calling out more evil spirits. The people were stunned. They had never encountered anyone like Jesus. Many people started following Him, and large crowds gathered wherever He went.

But people didn't always remain impressed by Jesus. Sometimes what Jesus said offended them and they stopped following Him. Other times, people got so upset that they tried to kill Him! But Jesus always escaped their evil plans. Nobody could stop Jesus—not the people who didn't understand Him, not the religious leaders who wanted to kill Him, and not the evil spirits. Jesus came from heaven for one reason, and He would accomplish God's plan no matter what.

BIG TRUTH

We are only saved through faith in Jesus.

Jesus' miracles and teaching amazed people, and many people followed Him wherever He went. But Jesus had a reason for teaching with authority and performing miracles; it wasn't to impress humans. Jesus' miracles and teachings revealed that He was the Messiah, God's promised rescuer. Jesus came into the world to accomplish God's plan. His was a mission of love. He would sacrifice Himself for our sins by dying on the cross and rising again from the grave. We are only saved through faith in Jesus.

BIG QUESTIONS

- How do you think it would have felt to be in the synagogue when Jesus was teaching? How about on the day when He cast out the evil spirit?

- Why does it matter that Jesus has power over evil spirits? Do you believe He still has that power over evil today?

- Are you impressed by Jesus? What is the most amazing thing about Jesus to you?

32

JESUS, THE STORM-CALMING SAVIOR

MATTHEW 8:23–27; MARK 4:35–41; LUKE 8:22–25

Wherever Jesus went, huge crowds of people came to see Him. When they came, He taught for long hours and did many miracles. One evening, when He was finished teaching, Jesus told His disciples to get into a boat so they could all go to the other side of the sea. Jesus was very tired, and as soon as they set sail, He fell asleep.

Suddenly, a powerful storm arose—one unlike anything Jesus' disciples had ever seen. Many of Jesus' disciples were experienced fishermen and had sailed through storms before, but this one was different. Waves crashed into the boat, which was filling with water faster than they could bail it out.

Meanwhile, Jesus slept.

The disciples, filled with fear, frantically woke Him up. "Lord!" they said. "We are going to die—don't you care? Save us!"

Jesus got up. The wind and the waves continued to rage around Him. Jesus looked at His desperate disciples. Then He asked, "Why are you afraid? Where is your faith?"

Why were the disciples afraid? How could Jesus ask this in the middle of this powerful storm? Surely He could see why! They thought they were all going to drown! And what did Jesus mean by asking them about their faith? He couldn't mean they didn't have any faith—they had left their entire lives behind to follow Him.

But before any of the disciples could answer Jesus' questions, He turned back to the sea, looked out at the water, and said, "Stop! Be still!" Then, just as suddenly as the storm came upon them, the water calmed down. But it wasn't just calm like a typical day; there wasn't even a ripple. Everything was perfectly still.

As scared as the disciples had been during the storm, they were even more terrified now. Clearly, the man they were with wasn't an ordinary human. An ordinary human, even a great and powerful prophet like Moses or Elijah had been, couldn't do what Jesus had just done. These people could perform certain miracles with God's help. But Jesus controlled nature itself—something only God Himself could do.

"What kind of man is this?" they asked. "Even the winds and the sea obey Him!"

"What kind of man is this? Even the winds and the sea obey Him!"

BIG TRUTH

As the Son of God, Jesus is both fully God and fully human.

As a human being, Jesus did all the things people do: He ate, drank, laughed, and slept. But Jesus isn't just a human being. Jesus is also fully God and can do the things only God can do. He has power over evil spirits, heals people, and rules over creation. Because Jesus is fully human, He understands everything you go through. Because He is fully God, He sustains the universe and reigns over it. There is no one like Jesus!

BIG QUESTIONS

- How do you think you would have felt during the storm? Do you think you would have woken Jesus up?

- Why do you think Jesus was sleeping soundly even as the wind and waves beat against the boat?

- When Jesus calmed the storm, He proved that He could control nature, something only God can do. What are some other ways Jesus does what only God can do?

33

JESUS, THE POWERFUL HEALER

MATTHEW 9:18–31; MARK 5:21–43; LUKE 8:40–56

Do you know one of the worst things a parent can imagine? Having a sick child and not being able to help! Has this ever happened in your family? Have you or one of your siblings gotten so sick that your parents couldn't make things better? If so, your parents probably understand what a man named Jairus felt like.

Jairus was one of the leaders in a synagogue in Galilee, and he had a very sick daughter he could not save. Then he heard the news: Jesus was in Galilee! At the time, Jesus was becoming more popular with the people because His miracles and teachings were like no one else's. They were different, special. So Jairus ran to meet Him.

When he saw Jesus, Jairus fell down at His feet. "Please, help my daughter!" he begged. "She is only twelve, and she's dying."

Who is this man who can do things only God can do?

Jesus agreed to help and went with Jairus. But there was a problem: the crowd around them kept growing. People were everywhere, pressed up against them. The walking was slow, but they plodded on.

Then Jesus stopped. "Who touched me?" He asked. His disciples thought this was strange. Considering the size of the crowd, maybe Jesus should have asked who hadn't touched Him! But Jesus kept asking. Some of His power had gone out of Him. This meant that someone in the crowd had been healed.

Just then, an older woman approached Jesus. She had been very ill for a long time, and no doctor could help her. She was so certain that even touching His clothes could help her somehow, she had reached out and grabbed His cloak. Immediately, she had been cured!

Jesus listened to her story, smiled, and said, "Go in peace. Your faith has made you well."

Just then, someone came from Jairus's house to deliver the sad news: his daughter had died. There was no need for Jesus to come. Jairus was heartbroken, but Jesus said, "Let's go! Don't be afraid. Only believe."

At Jairus's house, Jesus led Jairus, Jairus's wife, and His disciples to the girl. Grasping her hand, he said, "Time to get up, little girl." Immediately her eyes opened and she stood up and walked around. Jesus had brought her back from the dead!

Jesus healed many more people. Stories of His miracles spread throughout the area. Crowds grew everywhere He went, and people kept wondering: *Who is this man who can do things only God can do?*

BIG TRUTH

As the Son of God, Jesus is both fully God and fully human.

Jesus can do things that no ordinary human can. For example, while on earth, Jesus healed people, and He even did so without them asking. He knew things no one else knew—like when a single woman in a large crowd touched Him and believed she would be healed. Jesus even brought Jairus's daughter back to life, revealing His power over both life *and* death—a power that belongs only to God. As the Son of God, Jesus is both fully God and fully human.

BIG QUESTIONS

- How do you think the woman who was healed felt after all those years of illness? How do you think Jairus felt when he saw his daughter stand up and walk around?

- What do these healings teach you about Jesus?

- Why do you think having faith is so important to Jesus?

34

WHO BELONGS TO GOD'S KINGDOM?

MATTHEW 5:1–16

Whenever Jesus taught, people listened. He didn't teach like other teachers who sounded like they were just giving their opinions. Jesus taught with *authority*, or power, as if the way He understood God's Word was the only way to understand it.

One of the most important things Jesus taught about was God's kingdom. He wanted people to know what the Kingdom was like and how it was more valuable than anything else. Jesus also taught about how the people who belong to God's kingdom are different.

One day, Jesus was teaching to a very large crowd on a mountain in Capernaum. While describing God's kingdom, Jesus didn't start with a list of rules to follow or behaviors to copy. He did something better.

He described the character of God's people. He started by calling them *blessed*, which means happy in God.

Jesus said, "The poor in spirit know they have nothing to offer God because of sin. They are blessed because the kingdom is theirs."

God's people are blessed because they belong to God.

Jesus went on to describe what their hearts are like: "They mourn, but they will be comforted. They are humble and will inherit the earth. They desire God's righteousness, and they will have it. They are pure in heart, and they will see God."

He described how God's people interact with others: "They are merciful because they are shown mercy. They are peacemakers, for they are sons and daughters of God. Even when they are treated unkindly and cruelly by others because of Me, they are still blessed."

These are the kinds of people you will find in God's kingdom. Because God blesses them, they will bless others. God's joy will overflow out of their lives.

"Don't hide who you are," Jesus explained. "You are the light of the world, meant for everyone to see. Don't hide your light! Put it on a lampstand so it can give light to others. When you do this, people will give thanks for what you do. They will see how amazing your heavenly Father is and worship Him."

Jesus taught a lot more about how the people in God's kingdom should live, but it all starts with this: God's people are blessed because they belong to God.

BIG TRUTH

Jesus taught about God and His kingdom. He taught that all Scripture is about Him.

When Jesus taught, He didn't give people a new set of rules to follow or behaviors to imitate. He understood that wouldn't work. Instead, He described the heart of God's people, which is a heart of faith and humility. Everyone who comes to Jesus with a humble spirit is blessed because their sins are forgiven and God's kingdom is theirs. God's people are a light interacting with others in a way that shows everyone how amazing Jesus is.

BIG QUESTIONS

- Is following rules easy for you? Why do you think Jesus' description of God's kingdom was not about following rules?

- Why do you think Jesus called God's people *blessed*? Do all the things in Jesus' list seem like they would lead to blessedness?

- If you believe in Jesus, He wants you to be a light in the world. How might you show people how Jesus has blessed you?

35

JESUS TAUGHT ABOUT GOD'S LOVE

LUKE 15:1–32

When Jesus taught about God and His kingdom, all kinds of people came to hear. It wasn't just the people who were in the synagogue every week. Outcasts in society, tax collectors, and those called "sinners" came to listen to Jesus. The religious leaders were bothered by this. They didn't understand why Jesus would let all these people near Him. One day, Jesus explained why by telling three parables about God's love. A *parable* is a short story that reveals the truth about God's kingdom.

First, Jesus compared the people coming to Him to a lost sheep and a lost coin. "Who wouldn't go out in search of these if you lost them?" Jesus asked. "And who wouldn't celebrate when they were found? In the same way, there is great joy in heaven—even the angels rejoice—when one sinner turns to God."

But Jesus didn't stop there. He told them an even more complicated story, one that showed just how much God loved people.

"A man had two sons. The younger was rebellious and demanded his inheritance. The father gave him what he asked for, and a few days later, his son took all his belongings and left for a distant country. There he spent everything he had, and eventually, he hired himself out to feed pigs. He was so poor that he longed to eat the pig's food. Soon, the son said to himself, 'My father's hired hands have more than enough to eat! I will return to him and ask him to be one of his workers.'

"But when the father saw his son coming down the road, he started running toward him. Before his

God welcomes all to turn away from their sin and come to Him.

son could even say a word, the father grabbed him, hugged him, and cried because he was so happy. He put a ring on his son's finger and held a feast to celebrate his return.

"The older son didn't join in the festivities. He remained in the field, angry that his father welcomed his younger brother back so easily. The father said, 'You have been with me this whole time, and everything I have is yours! Your brother was lost, but now he is found. We have to celebrate his return!'"

Jesus told this story because He knew the truth. Like the father in the parable, God welcomes all to turn away from their sin and come to Him.

BIG TRUTH

Jesus taught about God and His kingdom. He taught that all Scripture is about Him.

Jesus' parables showed how God loves people—even those who reject Him. He loves people even when they love sin so much that they seem lost. The greatest demonstration of God's love was Jesus coming into the world. John 3:16 tells us "God loved the world in this way: He gave his one and only Son, so that everyone who believes in him will not perish but have eternal life." Like the father who welcomed his son home, God welcomes everyone into His family who comes to Him, no matter where they've been or what they've done!

BIG QUESTIONS

- Why do you think the father was so quick to welcome his younger son home?

- Do you think the older son was right to be angry with his father for his kindness toward his younger brother? Why or why not?

- Do you ever feel lost or far away from God? How does this story encourage you?

36

"LAZARUS, COME OUT!"

JOHN 11:1–44; 12:9–11

It's hard to imagine what Mary and Martha felt while they waited. Their brother Lazarus was sick, and they had sent a messenger to find Jesus. They knew that if anyone could help Lazarus, it was Jesus! This wasn't just because Mary and Martha had seen Jesus perform miracles; He was also their good friend.

Mary and Martha waited. Hours became days, but Jesus didn't come. Had He not received their message? What was going on? Soon, Lazarus died. Mary and Martha cried as they wrapped their brother in cloth and buried him in a tomb. Why didn't Jesus come? Why didn't He save Lazarus?

Four days after Lazarus died, Jesus showed up. Martha went to Him. She knew her brother would still be alive if Jesus had been there. But she also knew that God answered Jesus' prayers. Jesus seemed to be very close to God.

"Your brother will live again," Jesus told Martha. Because of Jewish beliefs, Martha understood that Lazarus would rise again in the last days. (But Jesus wasn't talking about this future day. Jesus meant *that day*.) He also said, "Everyone who believes in Me, even if they die, will live forever." Martha believed Him.

Then she told her sister Mary that Jesus had come. Mary found Jesus, fell at His feet, and cried, "If you had been here, Lazarus would still be alive!"

When Jesus saw Mary and others grieving for Lazarus, He felt many things: He was sad because His friend was dead, and He was angry because sin had made suffering and death part of the world.

So Jesus wept.

Jesus also felt excited because of what was about to happen. "Take me to Lazarus," He insisted. At the tomb, He commanded that they remove the large stone covering the entrance.

"But he's been dead for days," Martha protested. "He stinks!"

"Trust Me," Jesus said. "You're going to see God's power." After Jesus prayed and thanked God, He shouted into the tomb, "Lazarus! Come out." Lazarus, still wrapped in cloth, walked out of the cave. He was alive!

"Trust Me," Jesus said. "You're going to see God's power."

Everyone was amazed. Many people believed that Jesus was the Son of God because of this miracle. But the religious leaders weren't happy. They thought Jesus was lying about being God's Messiah. As far as they were concerned, He was leading people *away* from God, and they planned to do something about it.

BIG TRUTH

People reject Jesus because everyone is born with a sin nature and wants to please themselves rather than obey God.

Jesus did things that no normal human could. He healed people, helped them to see, and even raised people from the dead. Not everyone believed in Jesus because of what He did—even when they saw it for themselves. Some people rejected Jesus back then, and many people still do today. People reject Jesus because everyone is born with a sin nature and wants to please themselves rather than obey God. When we believe in Jesus, God brings our spiritually dead hearts to life.

BIG QUESTIONS

- How do you think Martha and Mary felt when Lazarus died and Jesus had not come to save him?

- How do you think you would have reacted seeing Lazarus step out of the tomb that day?

- Spend some time memorizing John 11:25–26: "I am the resurrection and the life. The one who believes in me, even if he dies, will live. Everyone who lives and believes in me will never die." Do you believe this? If not, what do you believe?

37

THE KING COMES TO JERUSALEM

MATTHEW 21:1–11; MARK 11:1–11; LUKE 19:35–46; JOHN 12:12–19

The crowds in Jerusalem were excited. The *Passover* was only days away. This meant everyone was getting ready to celebrate how God had rescued the Israelites from slavery out of Egypt hundreds of years earlier.

Something was different about this Passover, though—especially for Jesus' disciples. For about three years, Jesus had been teaching about God and His kingdom. But for several months, Jesus had been warning them that when they went to Jerusalem, He would be arrested and killed! The disciples didn't understand. After all, Jesus was the One God's people had been waiting for: He was the long-awaited Messiah, the rescuer, the king of Israel. How could He die before He set the people free from the Roman Empire?

When Jesus arrived in Jerusalem, the crowds shouted for joy. They laid their cloaks

and palm leaves along the road—a sign that they viewed Jesus as their king. Jesus, the humble servant that He was, rode into the city on a donkey.

"Blessed is he who comes in the name of the Lord," the people said. "The Son of David has come—our salvation is here!" They knew this moment was special. *Maybe now*, people thought, *Israel will be restored, just like God has promised.*

The religious leaders didn't like what was happening, and they didn't understand it. They demanded that Jesus tell His disciples to stop calling Him the Son of David. Jesus refused and said that if the people stopped, the rocks would cry out and start worshipping Him.

Then, as Jesus looked at the people and the city, He began to cry. He knew what must happen. The crowds, even His own disciples, didn't understand. They believed Jesus was going to defeat their Roman enemies. They thought Jesus would be a mighty warrior in battle like many of the Jewish kings before Him. But Jesus had come for a different reason. They just couldn't see it yet.

Even though Jesus *was* the King, He wasn't the king the people expected. Jesus is also God, so He knows what matters most. He sees the big picture. The people wanted Jesus to save them from the Roman Empire, but Jesus came to save them from a much greater problem: their sin.

When Jesus arrived in Jerusalem, the crowds shouted for joy.

BIG TRUTH

Jesus perfectly reveals God the Father and fulfills what the prophets spoke.

Throughout His life on earth, Jesus fulfilled prophecies about the Messiah, God's promised rescuer, and taught about what God is like. When Jesus came to Jerusalem riding on a donkey, He came as a humble King, and He did what the prophet Zechariah said He would do hundreds of years before (Zechariah 9:9). But Jesus didn't only enter Jerusalem as Messiah and King. He also came as *God*. Jesus is God in the flesh. Jesus perfectly reveals God the Father and fulfills what the prophets spoke in the Old Testament.

BIG QUESTIONS

- How do you think it would have felt to be in the crowd when Jesus arrived in Jerusalem? Do you think you would have cheered too?

- Throughout Jesus' time on earth, people didn't understand who Jesus was. Why do you think that was the case?

- It isn't just verses like Zechariah 9:9 that point to Jesus. Jesus said that the whole Bible speaks of Him (John 5:39). Can you find any other verses in the Old or New Testaments that are clearly about Jesus?

38

SYMBOLS OF JESUS' SACRIFICE

MATTHEW 26:17–30; MARK 14:12–26; LUKE 22:7–23

It was the night of the Passover. All over Jerusalem, the Jews were eating roasted lamb and unleavened bread, remembering the meal that their ancestors ate the night God delivered them from Egypt. Jesus and His disciples ate the meal together. But Jesus wasn't just eating it and remembering what God had done. Jesus was thinking about what He was going to do: lay down His life for the sins of the people.

As they prepared to eat, Jesus said to them, "One of you is going to betray me tonight."

The disciples were confused and very troubled. Betray Jesus? That didn't seem possible. They looked at one another. Then at Jesus. Then at one another again. One after the other, they asked the same question: "Is it me?"

Jesus already knew who was going to betray Him: Judas Iscariot. Judas was a thief, stealing from the group's money bag. Judas had already realized that Jesus was not the king he thought He would be. So Judas had gone to the religious leaders and agreed to betray Jesus for thirty pieces of silver.

Then Judas asked, "Is it me?"

Jesus said, "You have said so. Now go and do what you need to do."

Judas got up and left. The other disciples watched him leave, but they didn't understand what was happening. Then Jesus took bread from the meal and broke it. "Take this bread and eat it," He said. "This is my body, which is given for you. Remember Me whenever you eat it." After that, Jesus took a cup from the table and gave thanks.

"Take this cup and drink," He said. "This is my blood, which is poured out for you. Remember Me whenever you drink it."

The disciples ate and drank, not truly understanding what Jesus was saying. The bread and the cup were *symbols*, or visual representations, of what was about to happen to Jesus. Jesus was preparing to complete the work He came to do as the Son of God: saving people from sin by dying on the cross.

Jesus is the perfect sacrifice for our sins, and every time Christians take the bread and the cup during *Communion*, they remember Jesus loved us so much that He suffered on the cross and died in our place.

The bread and the cup were *symbols* of what was about to happen to Jesus.

BIG TRUTH

Jesus was the perfect sacrifice for sin, and He speaks to God the Father for us today.

When God's people celebrated the Passover, they remembered how God spared their ancestors from the final plague in Egypt. When they sacrificed a spotless lamb and painted their doorposts with its blood, death passed over their homes. But that sacrifice pointed forward to an even greater sacrifice: Jesus! Jesus came to earth to give His life away. Because He is God's Son who lived a sinless life, Jesus was the perfect sacrifice for sin, and He speaks to God the Father for us today. Today, all who believe in Jesus remember what He did when we take the bread and the cup during Communion.

BIG QUESTIONS

- How do you think you would have reacted when Jesus said one of the disciples would betray Him?

- Jesus didn't deserve to die on the cross, but He chose to anyway. What does this show you about Him?

- Today, Christians continue to remember Jesus' sacrifice for us by taking Communion. What questions do you have about the symbols of the bread and the cup?

39

"DO WHAT YOU HAVE COME TO DO."

MATTHEW 26:36–56; MARK 14:32–42; LUKE 22:39–53

After Jesus and the disciples ate the Passover meal, they went to a garden called Gethsemane. Jesus told Peter, James, and John to follow Him into the garden while the others waited outside. Jesus looked different to His disciples. He was troubled and sad, but in a way they had never seen before.

"Stay here, remain awake, and pray," Jesus told them before He went a little farther away, knelt down, and began to pray by Himself.

"Father, if you are willing, take this cup away from me," Jesus said. By this, Jesus was saying, "If there is any other way to forgive people's sins, can We do that instead?" Jesus added to His prayer, "Nevertheless, not My will, but Yours be done." Then He returned to Peter, James, and John, who had fallen asleep.

"Wake up," Jesus said. "Can't you stay awake to pray for even an hour?"

Jesus left them again to pray by Himself. Jesus was very distressed about dying on the cross. He knew the pain it would cause both His body and His spirit. He knew He would have to accept God's punishment against sin, and this was a distressing thought. So again, Jesus asked the Father, "If you are willing, take this cup from Me."

Then He went back to His disciples and found them sleeping again. Peter, James, and John were too weak to support Him, but Jesus found His strength in God and continued to pray.

Jesus returned to His disciples and had to wake them up again. Then a large mob with swords and clubs headed their way. Leading the mob was Judas Iscariot, one of Jesus' original twelve disciples. Judas went to Jesus and kissed Him—the sign of his betrayal—and the guards took hold of Jesus.

"I was with you every day in the temple, and you never touched me. But now you're arresting me as if I were a criminal?" Jesus said. "But do what you've come to do."

After Jesus' arrest, all His disciples ran away and abandoned Him. But Jesus left the garden differently than how He had entered it. He wasn't troubled in the same way. The plan of salvation wasn't going to change, and Jesus was determined that His Father's will would be done.

Jesus found His strength in God and continued to pray.

BIG TRUTH

Jesus was the perfect sacrifice for sin, and He speaks to God the Father for us today.

God answered Jesus' prayer with "No, there is no other way." By saying no to Jesus, God was saying yes to us. Because of what Jesus did, there is no sin God won't forgive when we come to Him. Jesus was the perfect sacrifice for sin, and He speaks to God the Father for us today. In the garden, Jesus modeled for us how to pray. We can ask God for what we want, trust that His will is best, and understand that if He says no, it's because He has a greater plan in mind.

BIG QUESTIONS

- Why do you think the disciples kept falling asleep when Jesus asked them to pray? Does it surprise you that Jesus wanted other people praying for Him?

- After asking God for what He wanted, Jesus prayed that the Father's will would be done, not His own. Have you ever tried praying like this?

- Imagine you had been with Jesus' disciples when the mob showed up to arrest Him. Do you think you would have run away too?

40

THE KING DIES

MATTHEW 27:27-56; MARK 15:16-41; LUKE 23:26-49; JOHN 19:16-37

The only way to describe what happened next is to call it the worst day ever. Jesus was taken to the religious leaders and then was treated cruelly by the Roman soldiers, who hit Him, mocked Him, and took Him away to be crucified. This was a terrible thing; it was the worst punishment someone could receive from the Romans. It was what only the worst of the worst criminals received.

But Jesus wasn't a criminal at all. Jesus was the Messiah, God's promised rescuer. He was the King of God's people.

On a hill outside of Jerusalem, Jesus was hung on His cross between two criminals. For hours, He stayed there, listening as people shouted insults at Him.

"If you're the king, save yourself!"

"He saved others, but He can't even save Himself!"

"Come down from the cross, and we'll believe You're the Messiah!"

Even the men hanging beside Jesus insulted Him, although one of them expressed faith in Him before the end.

Jesus did not respond to the people other than to pray, "Father, forgive them. They don't know what they're doing."

Despite His pain, Jesus *didn't* come down from the cross. He could have come down. He had the power to do it. But Jesus needed to stay there. His mission of love wasn't finished yet.

Later in the day, around noon, the sky became dark. For three hours, there was no light. And Jesus began to speak in a loud voice. "My God, my God," He said, "why have you abandoned me?"

Suddenly, the ground shook, and the curtain that separated God's presence from the people in the temple tore in two. Jesus cried out, "It is finished!" At last, God's plan was complete. Jesus said, "Father, into Your hands, I entrust My spirit."

Then He breathed one more breath and died.

A Roman soldier who was watching Jesus was amazed at everything he saw. He praised

God, saying, "This man really was the Son of God!"

The soldiers took Jesus' body down from the cross, and Joseph from Arimathea buried it in a tomb that he owned. The religious leaders sealed the tomb and posted guards at the entrance.

It was the worst day ever. Jesus was dead, and His body locked inside a tomb. But it wasn't going to stay that way, because Jesus wasn't going to stay that way either.

BIG TRUTH

Jesus perfectly rules over the universe as the King of kings.

When Jesus was crucified, the Roman soldiers put a sign above His head to mock Him that said, "This is the King of the Jews." Even though they didn't believe it, they were telling the truth about who Jesus is. He is the King of the Jews, the Messiah the prophets said would rescue God's people. Jesus was just on a rescue mission that nobody expected—a mission of love to save people from sin. There has never been anyone else like Jesus. Today, Jesus perfectly rules over the universe as the King of kings who deserves all our worship.

BIG QUESTIONS

- How do you think Jesus felt when people were insulting Him as He hung on the cross?

- What would have happened if Jesus had come off the cross to save Himself from the pain?

- How does this true story make you feel about Jesus? What does it show you about God?

41

JESUS IS ALIVE!

MATTHEW 27:57–28:15; MARK 15:42–16:8; LUKE 23:50–24:12; JOHN 19:38–20:10

It was the morning after the Sabbath. Mary Magdalene, one of Jesus' followers, still couldn't believe what had happened. How could Jesus be dead? He was the Messiah! The King of God's people couldn't really be gone, could He? Mary Magdalene remembered how Jesus talked about how He would die, but He would also rise again. Maybe that was really going to happen.

Wouldn't that be incredible?

Mary Magdalene and another woman named Mary walked to Jesus' tomb. The women were hoping to wrap Jesus' body in linen cloths and spices according to their customs since they didn't have time to do it all on the day He died. They hoped the guards in front of the tomb would let them in.

Suddenly, there was a powerful earthquake! Both women were terrified. The stone in front of the tomb had been rolled away, and an angel dressed all in white was sitting on the stone. Not surprisingly, the guards had fallen down in terror at the sight.

"Don't be afraid," one angel said to the women. "I know you're looking for Jesus. But look, He is not here! Come and see."

Both Marys looked inside the tomb. It was empty, just as the angel said. Jesus' body was gone.

"Now, go quickly and tell the disciples," the angel said. "They need to know that Jesus has risen from the dead—He is alive! He is going to Galilee and will see them there."

The women ran from the tomb, their hearts bursting with excitement. Jesus was alive! It seemed almost too good to be true— and then something even more amazing happened. Jesus appeared to them. When they saw Him, they fell down, grabbed His feet, and worshipped Him.

Jesus sent the women back to the other disciples to share the good news. Some of the disciples didn't believe it, but Peter and John got up and ran to the tomb. They found it empty, just like the women had said. Peter and John were amazed. Jesus was alive! He really was the Messiah. Everything He had ever said was true.

"Jesus has risen from the dead—He is alive!"

BIG TRUTH

Jesus perfectly rules over the universe as the King of kings.

When Jesus died on the cross, the religious leaders thought it was the end of Him. When they heard about His resurrection, they refused to believe it and even paid the soldiers who guarded the tomb money to lie about it. Today people still doubt that Jesus rose from the dead, but that doesn't mean it isn't true. Jesus' resurrection is real, and it's the best news ever. Because Jesus was the perfect sacrifice for sin, He didn't stay dead. He rose to life and is alive forever! Jesus perfectly rules over the universe as the King of kings.

BIG QUESTIONS

- How would you have felt if you had gone to Jesus' tomb that morning and seen it empty?

- Why do you think some of the disciples and the religious leaders refused to believe that Jesus was alive?

- How does Jesus being alive change your life forever? Who is someone you can tell about Jesus?

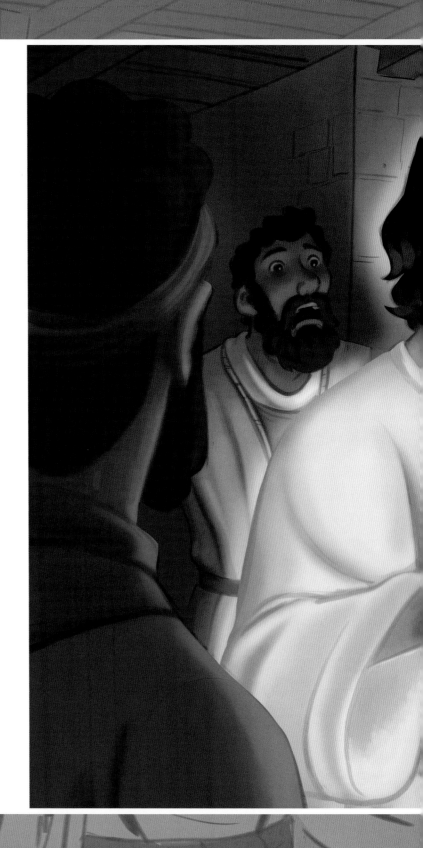

42

"IT'S REALLY ME!"

LUKE 24:13-49

*C*ould it really have been Jesus? Two disciples ran back to Jerusalem, their hearts burning with excitement. They felt more alive than they'd ever been. This feeling had been there ever since Jesus had met them on the road and explained to them how the Scriptures, from beginning to end, revealed who He was and what He was going to do.

When they found the other disciples, they all began to discuss what had happened. Jesus had just appeared to these two on the road. That meant that since He had risen from the dead, He had appeared to them *and* Peter *and* John *and* Mary Magdalene *and* the other Mary too. *How could this be?*

Suddenly, while everyone was talking, Jesus showed up. The disciples were terrified. Jesus hadn't been in the room a moment ago, and He hadn't walked through the door. Where had He come from? Was He a ghost?

"Why are you troubled? Don't be afraid—it really is Me!"

Knowing what the disciples were thinking, Jesus said, "Why are you troubled? Don't be afraid—it really is Me! Here, touch My hands. A ghost doesn't have flesh and blood like I do."

The disciples were astonished. Some touched His hands. Others just stood, too excited to believe what was happening.

"Do you have anything to eat?" He asked.

Wait—eat? Jesus was hungry? Maybe He really was alive. They gave Him a piece of broiled fish, and He ate it; they watched Jesus take every bite.

Then Jesus said to the disciples, "This is what I told you while I was still with you. Everything written about me in the Law of Moses, the Prophets, and the Psalms must be fulfilled." Then, just like He did on the road with the two disciples, Jesus explained how all the Scriptures, from beginning to end, revealed who He was and what He was going to do. The disciples were in awe. How had they never realized this before? How could they have not understood it until now?

But Jesus didn't stop with telling them about God's plan for Him; He also talked about God's plan for them. Jesus had suffered, died, and risen from the dead, and because of that, people's sins could be forgiven. *What would happen now?* Jesus explained that He would send His disciples into the world to share this incredible news with others!

BIG TRUTH

We can know that God wants us to know Him by the many ways He has revealed Himself to us, best of all through Jesus.

Jesus said, "The one who has seen Me has seen the Father" (John 14:9). Jesus was with God before anything else existed. He knows what God is like in a way no one else does. More than that, Jesus carried out God's great plan of love to save people from sin through His death and resurrection. The Bible is all about God's plan of salvation. Just like it was for the disciples, this is the good news we get to share with others!

BIG QUESTIONS

- Imagine you were with the disciples when Jesus appeared in the room. How do you think you would have reacted?

- Why is it important that Jesus wasn't a ghost or spirit after He rose again, but a flesh-and-blood human?

- God's entire plan of love was to save people from sin through Jesus. Why do you think it's hard for some people to believe this?

43

GO—BUT FIRST, WAIT FOR THE HOLY SPIRIT

ACTS 1:1–14

Jesus appeared to His disciples for forty days after His resurrection. Every time He appeared, He reminded them that He really was alive and talked to them about the kingdom of God. At the end of forty days, it was time for Jesus to return to heaven and be with God the Father. He took the core group of eleven disciples who remained to a mountain in Galilee.

Jesus said, "I am leaving you, but in a few days, the Holy Spirit will come to you. Wait in Jerusalem until He comes."

The disciples asked, "Lord, now are you going to restore the kingdom?"

Even now, the disciples *still* didn't understand what Jesus meant. They knew that Jesus was the Messiah, God's promised rescuer, and the long-awaited king from King David's family. But they *still* thought about Him the way many other Jews did. They thought that

the Messiah would be a king like other human kings—a military leader, a ruler of a nation. They thought Jesus would restore Israel, overthrow the Romans, and make them a great nation like they had been when other kings had reigned. But Jesus had something much more important in mind. Everything that sin had ruined needed to be restored. Jesus planned to make everything new through His spiritual kingdom.

"It's not the time for you to know when that will happen," Jesus said. "Wait for the Holy Spirit to come to you. When He does, He will give you the power to be My witnesses about God's kingdom. Tell everyone that God offers forgiveness for sin. Start with Jerusalem, then tell the Samaritans, and finally, go into all the world."

Then, as the disciples watched, Jesus began to rise up into the sky. He kept going higher and higher until a cloud covered Him. Then, He was gone. The disciples kept looking up. *What happened?* they wondered. *What are we supposed to do?*

The disciples left the mountain and went back to Jerusalem. Jesus was gone, but someday in the future He would come back. Before that happened, the Holy Spirit would arrive to help all who believe in Jesus spread the good news about Him.

"The Holy Spirit will give you the power to be My witnesses."

BIG TRUTH

The Holy Spirit comforts us, shows us our sin, and guides us as we live for God's glory.

Before Jesus returned to heaven, He promised that His disciples wouldn't be alone. He promised to send someone else to them: the Holy Spirit. The Holy Spirit comforts us, shows us our sin, and guides us as we live for God's glory. The Holy Spirit lives in the heart of every person who trusts in Jesus, helping us to obey God and tell others about how great Jesus is.

BIG QUESTIONS

- Why do you think Jesus kept insisting that He really was alive?

- How do you think the disciples felt on the mountain that day? How would you feel if you had to watch the person you loved most leave you?

- Jesus' first disciples didn't understand everything Jesus taught them—even though they heard it directly from His own mouth. What are some things you don't understand from the Bible?

44

THE HOLY SPIRIT CAME WITH POWER

ACTS 2

All of Jesus' disciples were in Jerusalem, where they'd been since Jesus went up into heaven. They were doing what Jesus told them to do: waiting. Jesus had promised the Holy Spirit would come—and when He did, the disciples would receive power. But it had been over a week already, and nothing had happened. Now it was the day of *Pentecost*, which was one of the Jewish people's annual harvest festivals. What would happen when the Holy Spirit arrived?

Without warning, there was a loud sound like a violent rushing wind. It filled the entire house where the disciples were staying. They saw something that looked like flames appear in the room, but it wasn't normal fire. Like the fire Moses saw in the wilderness, it didn't burn. The flame separated and rested on each of the disciples. They were all filled with the Holy Spirit! Each disciple began to speak in a

different language as the Spirit gave them the ability.

Out in the street, Jewish people from all over the world gathered. They heard the sound of the rushing wind and the disciples speaking in different languages, talking about the magnificent things God had done. They were bewildered. Why were their own languages being spoken? And the people speaking—these followers of Jesus—were Galileans, hardly the most educated or important people. What did all of this mean?

Peter spoke to the crowd. "What's happening now is what the prophet Joel said would happen: 'It will be in the last days, says God, that I will pour out My Spirit on all people'" (Joel 2:28–32). Peter told them about what happened to Jesus during the Passover, how He was killed but then rose again from the dead. "This man was the Messiah."

The people asked Peter, "What should we do?"

"Turn away from your sins, trust in Jesus, and be baptized. Then you will receive the Holy Spirit too." After Peter preached, three thousand people started to follow Jesus that day.

These people devoted themselves to the apostles' teaching, prayer, and living life with the other disciples. The believers shared all they had with one another, and their reputation grew throughout Jerusalem. Day after day, God added more people to those who trusted in Jesus.

"Turn away from your sins, trust in Jesus, and be baptized. Then you will receive the Holy Spirit too."

BIG TRUTH

The Holy Spirit comforts us, shows us our sin, and guides us as we live for God's glory.

When the Holy Spirit came to the disciples, He gave them the power they needed to fulfill their mission: to take the gospel into the world and make more disciples. But the Holy Spirit didn't just give them the power to share the gospel with their words. He gave them a new desire to serve and love one another. The disciples cared for one another and shared everything they had. In the same way today, the Holy Spirit binds all believers together. The Holy Spirit comforts us, shows us our sin, and guides us as we live for God's glory.

BIG QUESTIONS

- Imagine you were in the streets of Jerusalem when the Holy Spirit came to the disciples. How would you have reacted?

- How do you think the disciples felt when they saw so many people join them after Peter preached?

- If you believe in Jesus, what is one thing you need the Holy Spirit's help with today?

45
PETER'S FEARLESS PREACHING

ACTS 3–4

The early days of the apostles' ministry were exciting. The *apostles* were the people Jesus chose to be His special representatives. They included the twelve disciples, Saul (who became Paul), and Jesus' brothers James and Jude. They knew they had a mission—to go and tell people about Jesus—and they did it boldly.

One day, Peter and John went to the temple, where they taught that God offers forgiveness to anyone who believes in Jesus. Whenever they preached, more people believed the gospel.

The religious leaders weren't happy about this. They didn't believe Jesus was the Messiah. So when Peter and John healed a disabled man at the temple, they brought them to stand before the *Sanhedrin*, the ruling council of the Jewish people.

"There is no other name under heaven given to people by which we must be saved."

"How were you able to heal this man?" they asked. "Who gave you the power to do it?"

Peter, filled with the Holy Spirit, said, "If we are being examined because of this good deed, you need to know that it was done in the name of Jesus Christ—the man you crucified, but God raised from the dead. This man is healthy because of Jesus!"

Peter told the religious leaders that even though they rejected Jesus, He is the only way to salvation. "There is no other name under heaven given to people by which we must be saved," he said.

The religious leaders were stunned by Peter and John's boldness. After all, these men were poor, uneducated, and untrained. Still, they had performed an obvious miracle in Jesus' name—one so obvious they couldn't deny it.

There was nothing the Sanhedrin could do to punish Peter and John, so they released them and warned them to stop teaching about Jesus completely.

But Peter and John said, "Which is right: for us to obey God or to obey you? We can't stop speaking about what we have seen and heard." Then they left.

When they returned to the disciples, they shared what happened. All the people were amazed and prayed God would give them even more boldness to preach the gospel. God answered their prayer. The next time they departed, they were filled with power from the Holy Spirit and they continued to speak boldly about Jesus. As they did more miracles in His name, more and more people believed in Jesus.

BIG TRUTH

We tell others about Jesus so they will hear and believe the good news.

Even after Peter and John were arrested for preaching the gospel, they kept doing it anyway. It was more important for them to obey God than to obey people. We tell others about Jesus so they will hear and believe the good news of salvation. It's not always easy to do this, so we need to pray that God will give us power and boldness to speak about Jesus the way we should (Ephesians 6:19).

BIG QUESTIONS

- How do you think Peter and John felt when they were brought before the Sanhedrin?

- Do you think it's possible to be brave and scared at the same time? Why?

- Have you ever been afraid to talk about Jesus? Did you do it anyway? What happened?

46

A WISE WARNING

ACTS 5:12-42

As the apostles continued to talk about Jesus and more people kept joining them, the religious leaders got fed up. The high priest was jealous of them, so he had them arrested. When the high priest's servants went to the jail to bring the apostles before the Sanhedrin, they were shocked: the jail was empty even though the doors were locked. They didn't know that an angel had come to free the apostles. *How did this happen?* they wondered. *What does it mean?*

Then someone told the religious leaders, "Look! The men you put in jail are standing in the temple and teaching the people." So the guards grabbed the apostles and brought them before the Sanhedrin. The high priest asked, "Didn't we tell you to stop teaching about Jesus? You're filling Jerusalem with your teaching!"

Peter and the apostles replied the same way they did the last time they were in front of the religious leaders. "We must obey God

rather than people," they said. "God raised up Jesus, and you sent Him to die on a cross. But God made Him Ruler and Savior of all. Now all who believe will have forgiveness of sins. We have seen that these things are true. The Holy Spirit has too, because He is with everyone who obeys God!"

The religious leaders became so angry they wanted to kill the apostles. But a teacher named Gamaliel sent the apostles away and spoke to the other leaders. "Be careful about what you do to these men," he said. "Others have claimed to be the Messiah and it's come to nothing. If what these men are saying is untrue, the same will happen. But if it is of God, you cannot stop them. You might even be fighting against God."

The religious leaders were convinced for the time being, but they still had the apostles punished before sending them away.

"Stop talking about Jesus," they warned as they released them.

But the apostles didn't stop. They kept preaching about Jesus in the temple. They taught about Him in peoples' homes. Everywhere they went, they proclaimed the good news that Jesus is the Messiah who has come to rescue sinners and bring them into God's kingdom.

How did this happen? What does it mean?

BIG TRUTH

Jesus became human to obey His Father's plan and rescue sinners.

The religious leaders didn't believe the apostles' message about Jesus. They thought Jesus was an ordinary human being, not the Messiah. Many people today believe the same thing. They think Jesus was an ordinary person, but not God, and definitely not the Savior of the world. Even if people refuse to believe it, the apostles' message is still true: Jesus is the Messiah, God's promised rescuer. Every person, no matter who they are, who believes in Jesus will be saved.

BIG QUESTIONS

- How do you think the apostles felt when they were put in jail? How about when the angel came and freed them?

- If the religious leaders were right and Jesus wasn't the Messiah, do you think we would still be talking about Jesus more than 2,000 years later?

- If someone tells you to stop talking about Jesus, what should you do?

47
THE LEAST LIKELY CHRISTIAN EVER

ACTS 9:1–30

It's hard to imagine anyone who hated the Christians more than Saul. Saul was a *Pharisee*, a student of Jewish Law, and a well-known teacher. He was passionate about making sure the Jewish people only worshipped the God of Israel, and as far as He was concerned, Christians were leading people away from God.

So Saul began to persecute Christians, forcing all the disciples except for the apostles and a few others to leave Jerusalem. But that wasn't enough. Saul wanted to stop the message of Jesus completely. So he started hunting them down and arresting Christians.

One day, Saul and a group of men were traveling to Damascus with plans to arrest the Christians he found there. Suddenly, a light flashed around him, and he fell to the ground. He heard a voice come from the light:

"Saul, Saul, why are you persecuting me?"

"Who are you?" Saul said.

"I am Jesus," the voice said. "Go into Damascus, and you will learn what you must do."

The light disappeared. Saul got up, but he discovered that he couldn't see—he was blind! The other men had to lead him to Damascus.

There was a godly man named Ananias living in Damascus. Jesus had appeared to him and said, "Ananias, get up and go to a house on Straight Street. You'll find a man named Saul there. Place your hands on him so he may regain his sight."

Ananias was concerned. He had heard about Saul and the terrible things he did to Jesus' disciples. But Jesus said, "This man is my chosen instrument to take my name to Gentiles, kings, and Israelites. I will show him how much he must suffer for my name." So Ananias obeyed. He found Saul, put his hands on him, and prayed. At once, something fell from Saul's eyes, and his sight returned. Then Saul got up and was baptized.

Immediately, Saul was different! He went to the synagogues in Damascus and started to proclaim the truth that Jesus was the Son of God. Everyone who heard him was amazed. "Wait—isn't this the man who used to *arrest* Jesus' disciples?" they asked.

Even though people had doubts about him, Saul kept teaching that Jesus was the Messiah. He had been spiritually blind for a long time, but now he saw the truth. He had met Jesus! Because Saul knew Jesus, nothing was going to stop him from sharing the gospel.

Now Saul saw the truth. He had met Jesus!

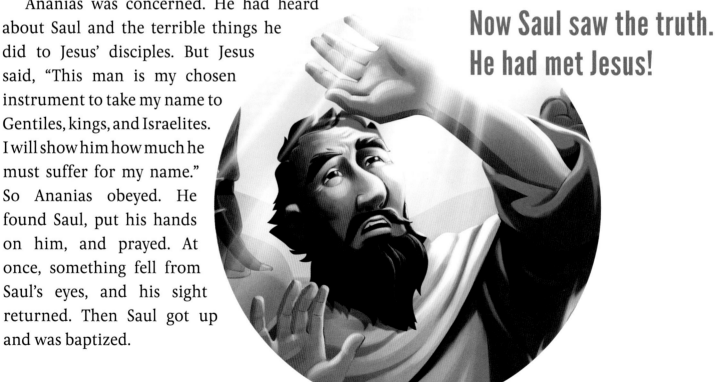

BIG TRUTH

Anyone who trusts in Jesus can be forgiven of their sins and be right with God.

People had a hard time believing that what happened to Saul was real. They had a hard time believing that he truly trusted Jesus. Even the apostles in Jerusalem weren't sure. After all, Saul had done too many terrible things to Christians! But anyone who trusts in Jesus can be forgiven of their sins and made right with God. Even though Saul was the least likely person to become a Christian, he had big faith in Jesus. God used him to teach many people that Jesus is the Messiah.

BIG QUESTIONS

- Imagine you were Ananias and you were told to go see Saul. How would you have felt? What would you have done?

- Why do you think people had a hard time believing that Saul truly believed in Jesus?

- Think of the person you know who is the least likely to trust in Jesus. Start praying that Jesus would save him or her.

48

THE GOSPEL IS FOR ALL

ACTS 10:1-43

One of the most important questions the first Christians had to answer was this: *Who is the gospel for?* The first disciples were all Jewish. They worshipped the God of Israel, and they knew Jesus was the Messiah. But God's plan was never to save only the Jews. God had saved Rahab, Ruth, the Ninevites, and others throughout the Old Testament. The gospel is for all people. The apostles just didn't understand that yet.

There was a man named Cornelius who lived in Caesarea. He was a *Gentile,* or a non-Jewish person, who worshipped God and prayed to Him. One day as he prayed, an angel told Cornelius to bring a man named Peter to his home.

The next day, Peter had a vision while traveling to a city called Joppa. He saw what looked like a large sheet coming down from the sky.

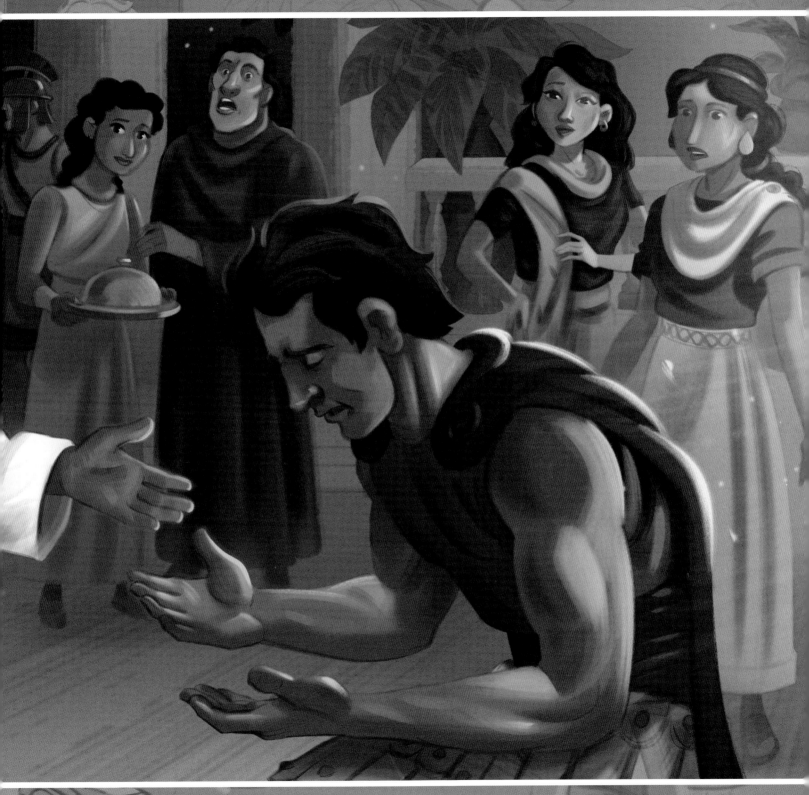

On it were all kinds of animals, birds, and reptiles, including ones the Law said Jewish people couldn't eat because they were impure or unclean.

A voice said to Peter, "Get up and eat."

Peter refused. "I have never eaten anything unclean." The voice said, "What God has made clean, do not call unclean." Then the sheet and animals were taken into heaven.

Peter was confused. What could the vision mean? As he considered it, three men sent by Cornelius called out to Peter. The Holy Spirit told him, "Go with these men. I have sent them to you." When Peter arrived at Cornelius's house, Cornelius began to worship him.

"Stop that!" Peter said. "I am a man just like you. But why did you send for me? Jewish men aren't supposed to visit with foreigners. Still, God has just shown me that I shouldn't call anyone impure or unclean."

Cornelius explained his vision, how an angel had appeared and told him to find a man named Peter. "Please, tell me everything you have been commanded by God," Cornelius begged.

So Peter explained the gospel to Cornelius, and he and everyone in his house believed.

Who is the gospel for? It is for the whole world!

Now Peter understood his vision! God was showing Peter that people from every nation who trust and obey Jesus are made clean before Him and welcomed into the Kingdom. The gospel came to the Jews, but it was also for the *Gentiles*, or non-Jewish people. *Who is the gospel for?* It is for the whole world!

BIG TRUTH

The church is all Christians everywhere who gather together in their communities to worship and serve God.

The gospel came to the Jewish people first, but it was never meant just for them. Jesus wanted His good news of salvation shared with people of all nations. God's people—the church—are not limited to one language, race, or nation. The gospel is for people of every country, language, culture, and ethnicity! Jesus' church is a global church. The *church* is all Christians everywhere who gather together in their communities to worship and serve God.

BIG QUESTIONS

- Peter was confused about his vision at first. How do you think Peter felt when he realized what his vision meant?

- Why is it good news that the gospel isn't just for one group of people, but for everyone?

- Christians around the world worship God in different ways. How might you learn about different ways Christians worship God around the world?

49

SHARING THE GOSPEL WHEREVER WE GO

ACTS 15:36–18:22

After Saul, who was also called Paul, became a Christian and an apostle of Jesus, he made several journeys as a missionary, traveling to different cities to teach people about Jesus. At first, Paul visited the Jewish synagogues, but they kicked him out. So he began teaching the Gentiles, or non-Jewish people, instead. The Gentiles began to trust in Jesus!

During these journeys, Paul traveled with different ministry partners. One was a man named Silas. Paul and Silas went to a city called Thyatira. One day, while they were on their way to pray, a girl met them in the street. She had a spirit in her that she used to predict the future. For days she followed them around shouting that they were servants of God proclaiming a way of salvation. (Even though what she said was true, she was saying it so that people would not believe Paul and Silas' message.)

The gospel continued to spread, and nothing and nobody could stop it.

Paul was patient with the girl at first, but he soon became annoyed and commanded the spirit to leave the girl in the name of Jesus. The spirit left immediately. Now, the people the girl worked for weren't happy about this. (With the spirit gone, how would they make any money telling fortunes?) So they attacked Paul and Silas. More people—and even the police!—joined in as well, hitting them with rods and throwing them in jail.

That night, Paul and Silas prayed and sang hymns to God while the other prisoners listened. Suddenly a violent earthquake shook the jail until all the doors were opened and all the chains came loose. When the jailer saw what happened, he planned to harm himself because he thought he would get in trouble for the prisoners' escape. But Paul shouted, "Don't hurt yourself—we're all here!" The jailer couldn't believe it. He took Paul and Silas out of the prison and asked, "What must I do to be saved?"

"Believe in the Lord Jesus and you will be saved," they said. They shared the gospel with him and with everyone in his home, and they all believed and were baptized.

After they left Thyatira, Paul and Silas traveled to Thessalonica, Berea, Athens, and Corinth. Everywhere they went, they found that some people stood against them, but many people believed the good news about Jesus. They started churches and encouraged Christians to keep their faith. The gospel continued to spread, and nothing and nobody could stop it.

BIG TRUTH

Our mission is to make disciples of all nations by the power of the Holy Spirit.

Paul and his ministry partners understood that the gospel wasn't just for the Jews, but for all people. They traveled all over the Mediterranean and into Asia teaching about Jesus and starting new churches. Those churches then started new churches, which sent out more people to teach about Jesus. We are a part of the same mission that Paul was a part of back then. Our mission is to make disciples of all nations by the power of the Holy Spirit. Just like Paul, we share God's love and message wherever we go.

BIG QUESTIONS

- Do you think it was easy for Paul and Silas to keep teaching about Jesus when the people were against them? Why or why not?

- Why do you think Paul and Silas were able to sing songs while in prison?

- There are many countries where very few Christians—or none at all—exist. Pray that God would send missionaries to these countries to continue to spread the wonderful news about Jesus. Ask God if He wants to send you one day.

50

A STORM-TOSSED JOURNEY

ACTS 27–28

Paul traveled the world as a missionary for many years. He started many churches and wrote letters to encourage and teach Christians. But there was one city where he wanted to go to share the gospel more than any other: Rome, the capital of the Roman Empire. When Paul finally went, it wasn't as a missionary. It was as a prisoner.

On his final trip to Jerusalem, Paul was attacked by a mob who began to tell lies about what he was teaching. Paul went before the Sanhedrin, then the governor, and even King Agrippa. Finally, he asked to be seen by Caesar, the powerful Roman emperor. Paul had the right to ask this because he was a Roman citizen.

The journey to Rome wasn't easy. The voyage was slow because the ship made several stops. After many weeks of travel, the crew decided it would be best to turn back

and spend the winter on the island of Crete. Paul warned the men that disaster was ahead, but no one listened to him. They kept sailing and made it to Crete.

Soon, a strong wind came from the island and forced them to set sail again. For days, the ship was tossed by the storm. The sailors began to throw the cargo overboard to try to stay afloat. The crew struggled to keep the ship under control, and everyone began to give up hope.

Paul said, "You should have listened to me and not gone to Crete. We would have avoided all this damage and loss. Now, take courage! An angel of God told me last night that we will survive, and I will appear before Caesar. The only thing that will be lost on this trip is the ship itself. Now, we must run aground on an island."

Paul warned the men that disaster was ahead.

The ship crashed on an island called Malta, just as Paul said. The ship was destroyed, but all 276 sailors survived. Paul prayed for the people on the island, healed the sick, and told them about Jesus. When they left three months later, the people of Malta were sad to see them go and gave them all they needed to finish their journey to Rome.

Finally, after months of traveling, Paul arrived in Rome, as a prisoner. For two years, he stayed by himself under house arrest. Many people from Rome came to visit him—both Jews and Gentiles. Paul taught them about Jesus' death, resurrection, and eventual return to earth. No one tried to stop him.

BIG TRUTH

We should praise Jesus for what He has done to provide our salvation and also because He is returning one day to make all things right.

When Paul arrived in Rome, he thanked God for protecting him on the difficult journey and for doing what He said He would do. God promised Paul he would make it to Rome, and he did. God promised Paul he would stand before Caesar, and he did. Paul trusted all of God's promises, including Jesus' promise to return to earth one day as King. Today, we should praise Jesus for what He has done to provide our salvation and also because He is returning one day to make all things right.

BIG QUESTIONS

- Why do you think Paul kept serving God even though his life as a Christian was hard?

- What does this story teach you about God? What does it teach you about following God?

- Paul's praise of God was based on God's promises. What is a promise you want to thank Him for?

51
A VISION OF THE THRONE

REVELATION 4–5

What do you think heaven is like? You might have picked up some ideas about heaven from church or other books, but did you know the Bible actually tells us what it's like?

When the apostle John was very old, Jesus gave him a vision of the future. He showed John many things, including a glimpse of heaven. John saw a throne with someone sitting on it that he couldn't even describe—the Lord—and beside Him was a scroll. Around His throne were twenty-four thrones on which sat twenty-four men, each dressed in white and wearing a golden crown. They all worshipped the One on the throne in the center. John saw four creatures he couldn't even name, who had many eyes, many wings, and different faces like a lion, human, eagle, and ox. Day and night, the creatures said,

"Holy, holy, holy,
Lord God, the Almighty,
who was, who is, and who is to come."
– Revelation 4:8

But it wasn't just the living creatures or the elders, or even the Lord Himself. There was another who looked like a lamb—Jesus. Jesus took the scroll from the hand of God, and when He did, the men on the thrones began to worship Jesus, saying:

"You are worthy to take the scroll . . .
You purchased people
for God by your blood
from every tribe and language
and people and nation.

"You made them a kingdom
and priests to our God,
and they will reign on the earth."
—Revelation 5:9–10

The men were joined by more voices worshipping Jesus, the Lamb. Countless thousands of angels began to say loudly,

"Worthy is the Lamb who was slaughtered
to receive power and riches
and wisdom and strength
and honor and glory and blessing!"
—Revelation 5:12

And then John heard even more voices—voices from every creature in heaven and on earth, all saying,

"Blessing and honor and glory and power
be to the one seated on the throne,
and to the Lamb, forever and ever!"
—Revelation 5:13

Jesus is worthy of all praise!

Jesus is the Lamb that the angels, creatures, and people will worship forever. Jesus became a sacrifice for us in the most loving act the world has ever seen. One day, Jesus will return to make all things right. We worship Jesus today, and we will worship Him forever. Jesus is worthy of all praise!

BIG TRUTH

The church looks forward to Jesus' return when He will make all things new.

We get to worship Jesus now on earth, praising Him for who He is and how He has saved us. But our worship now is only a small taste of what we will experience when Jesus returns. When He does, we will see Him face-to-face. We will celebrate with all of creation and finally worship Him the way He deserves—with our whole hearts, forever. The church looks forward to Jesus' return when He will make all things new.

BIG QUESTIONS

- What is most exciting to you about John's vision of God's throne room?

- Why does John see Jesus as a Lamb in his vision? What has Jesus done for us?

- What are some ways you can worship Jesus now while we wait to worship Him forever?

52

THE ENDING WE'RE WAITING FOR

REVELATION 19–22

Sometimes people think that if you know how a story will end, the story is ruined. But the Bible is not that way. Knowing the end of the story is what makes the whole thing great news!

In the book of Revelation, Jesus showed the apostle John a vision of the future, or images of what will happen when Jesus returns to earth. John saw a rider on a white horse, who was Jesus, the King of kings and Lord of lords. King Jesus rode into battle against a powerful beast who pretended to be the ruler of the world. Even though the beast and its army were powerful, Jesus defeated them once and for all. He bound the beast, and then on the day of judgment, cast it into the lake of fire, never to return.

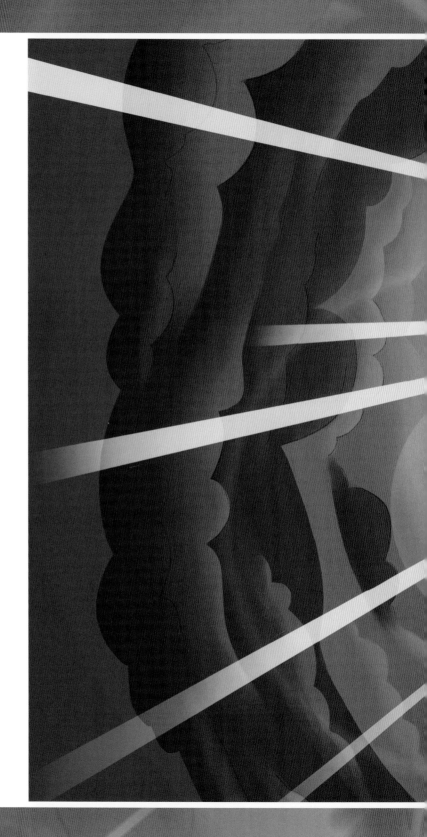

We don't need to wonder if Jesus wins. We already know He does!

Then John saw a new heaven and a new earth come into being—a new world where people of every nation, ethnicity, and language will live together with God in the heavenly city, the new Jerusalem. Sickness, sadness, and suffering will be no more. Death will not exist. There will be no temple because Jesus will be the temple. There will be no sun nor moon because God's glory will be the light. And best of all, God's people will live with God, face-to-face, forever.

This is the ending that makes the Bible's story so good. We don't need to wonder if Jesus wins. We already know He does! We know sin is going to be undone. We know death will be defeated. Knowing the end of the story means we can have hope, even during our hardest and darkest days on earth. And best of all, we know the end of the story is coming soon. Jesus *will* return. He will make all things new, and everyone who trusts in Him will get to enjoy life with Him for eternity!

BIG TRUTH

The church looks forward to Jesus' return when He will make all things new.

One day, Jesus is going to put an end to all sin, sadness, and suffering. He is going to undo death once and for all. Then all who believe in Him will get to live with Him forever! The promise of Jesus' return is what gives us hope to share His story with others. There isn't a question of *what* is going to happen. The only question is *when* it will happen. Jesus, the King of kings and Lord of lords, is coming back!

BIG QUESTIONS

- How does knowing that Satan (the beast) and his armies lose in the end make you feel?

- How does knowing that Jesus will restore everything that is broken make you feel?

- How do you want to live while we wait for Jesus to return?

apostles (n). The people whom Jesus chose to be His special representatives. They included the twelve disciples, Saul (who became Paul), and Jesus' brothers James and Jude. The *apostles'* mission was to go and tell people about Jesus and teach with His authority. (pg. 186)

ark (n). A massive boat. (pg. 24)

authority (n). The power or right to speak or act. (pg. 142)

baptize (v). To dip someone under water and bring them up again as a sign of their repentance and desire to live a new life in Jesus. (pg. 122)

blessed (adj). To be happy in God. (pg. 142)

church (n). all Christians everywhere who gather together in their communities to worship and serve God. (pg. 201)

Communion (n). Christians remember Jesus' sacrifice on the cross by taking the bread and the cup as part of *Communion.* (pg. 160)

covenant (n). A commitment or a promise. (pg. 76)

decree (n). An order that must be obeyed. (pg. 106)

dedicate (v). To set apart for God. (pg. 82)

disciple (n). A student or follower. For example, Jesus' *disciples* followed Him wherever He went, learned from Him, and helped Him in His ministry. (pg. 126)

exile (n). An extended time away from one's homeland. (pg. 102)

faithful (adj). To be steady, constant, and trustworthy. (pg. 37)

family redeemer (n). In Bible times, someone who could protect the members of a family. In the case of Boaz and Ruth, Boaz married Ruth and purchased Naomi's husband's land as the *family redeemer.* (pg. 64)

Gentile (n). A non-Jewish person. (pg. 198)

grace (n). Doing good for someone when they don't deserve it. (pg. 70)

heir (n). In Bible times, the son who would inherit the family property. (pg. 26)

holy (adj). Pure and perfect in every way. (p.69)

idol (n). A false god. (pg. 86)

idolatry (n). A sin of the heart in which humans love and value something else other than the one true God. (pg. 89)

Immanuel (n). A name for Jesus that means "God with us." (pg. 118)

Israel (n). The name of the northern kingdom of Israel after Solomon died and the kingdoms were divided. (pg. 86)

Jew (n). A name given to God's people because they were from the land of Judah. (pg. 110)

Judah (n). The name of the southern kingdom of Israel after Solomon died and the kingdoms were divided. (pg. 86)

living water (n). Eternal life with God. (pg. 128)

mercy (n). Not punishing someone when they deserve it. (pgs. 81, 84)

Messiah (n). The rescuer God promised; Jesus. (pgs. 76, 116)

miracle (n). Something God does that usually cannot be done so we can know He is all-powerful. (pg. 57)

parable (n). A short story that reveals the truth about God's kingdom. (pg. 146)

Passover (n). A celebration of God's deliverance of the Israelites from slavery out of Egypt. (pgs. 40, 154)

Pentecost (n). In Bible times, an annual Jewish harvest festival. In modern times, Christians celebrate *Pentecost* as the coming of the Holy Spirit. (pg. 182)

Pharisee (n). a student of the Jewish law (pg. 194)

prophet (n). A messenger from God. (pg. 86)

repent (v). To turn away from one's sin and turn to Jesus. (pgs. 93, 122)

Sanhedrin (n). The ruling council of the Jewish people. (pg. 186)

sin (v). To think, say, or behave in any way that goes against God and His commands. (pg. 18)

symbol (n). A visual representation. For example, the cup and the bread are *symbols* for Jesus' sacrifice because of what happened to His body when He died on the cross. (pg. 160)

synagogue (n). A place of worship and learning about God. (pg. 130)

worship (n). The act of celebrating the greatness of God, which often involves singing and praise. (pg. 42)

BIG TRUTH VERSES

The Big Truths throughout this book were not made up; the concepts come straight from the Bible. Do you want to take these Big Truths with you wherever you go? Then challenge yourself to memorize these Big Truth Verses. Recite them to your family members. Invite a friend to memorize them with you. Most important, ask God to help you believe and act on these big messages!

God created everything for His glory and our good. (Stories 1, 2)

From him and through him and to him are all things. To him be the glory forever. Amen.—Romans 11:36

To sin is to think, say, or behave in any way that goes against God and His commands. (Stories 3, 4)

It is sin to know the good and yet not do it. —James 4:17

God is in control of everything in heaven and on earth. Nothing is outside of God's good plan. (Stories 5, 6)

We know that all things work together for the good of those who love God, who are called according to his purpose.—Romans 8:28

God always keeps His promises because He is faithful. (Stories 7, 8)

Let us hold on to the confession of our hope without wavering, since he who promised is faithful.—Hebrews 10:23

Worship is celebrating the greatness of God. (Story 9)

The LORD is great and is highly praised; he is feared above all gods.—Psalm 96:4

God is holy, good, and loving. (Story 10)

"I am the LORD, showing faithful love, justice, and righteousness on the earth, for I delight in these things."—Jeremiah 9:24

The Bible is God's Word that tells us what is true about God and ourselves. (Story 11)

The entirety of your word is truth, each of your righteous judgments endures forever.—Psalm 119:160

A miracle is something God does that usually cannot be done so that we can know He is all-powerful. (Story 12)

God also testified by signs and wonders, various miracles, and distributions of gifts from the Holy Spirit according to his will.—Hebrews 2:4

The fair payment for sin is death. (Stories 13, 14)

The wages of sin is death, but the gift of God is eternal life in Christ Jesus our Lord.—Romans 6:23

Because God is holy, sin has broken our relationship with God. (Story 15)

The wicked will not stand up in the judgment, nor sinners in the assembly of the righteous.—Psalm 1:5

Grace is when God gives us something good even when we do not deserve it. (Stories 16, 17)

You are saved by grace through faith, and this is not from yourselves; it is God's gift—not from works, so that no one can boast.—Ephesians 2:8–9

Mercy is when God does not give us the punishment we deserve. (Stories 18, 19)

God, who is rich in mercy, because of his great love that he had for us, made us alive with Christ even though we were dead in trespasses.—Ephesians 2:4–5

Idolatry is a sin of the heart in which we love and value something else above God. (Story 20)

"Do not have other gods besides me. Do not make an idol for yourself . . . Do not bow in worship to them, and do not serve them."—Exodus 20:3–5

Repentance is turning away from sin and turning to Jesus. (Story 21)

If we confess our sins, [God] is faithful and righteous to forgive us our sins and to cleanse us from all unrighteousness.—1 John 1:9

People are special because we are made in God's image, as male and female, to know Him. (Stories 22, 23)

God created man in his own image; he created him in the image of God; he created them male and female. —Genesis 1:27

God is in all places at all times and is always with His people. (Story 24)

"Can a person hide in secret places where I cannot see him?"—the LORD's declaration. "Do I not fill the heavens and the earth?"—the LORD's declaration.—Jeremiah 23:24

God cannot lie or ever be wrong, so we can trust whatever He has said. (Story 25)

God is not a man, that he might lie, or a son of man, that he might change his mind.—Numbers 23:19

When we sin, we should feel sorry that we have disobeyed God and want to turn from our sin because we love Him. (Stories 26, 27)

God, create a clean heart for me and renew a steadfast spirit within me.—Psalm 51:10

Jesus lived a sinless life, died on the cross, and rose from the dead. (Stories 28, 29)

I passed on to you as most important what I also received: that Christ died for our sins according to the Scriptures, that he was buried, that he was raised on the third day according to the Scriptures.—1 Corinthians 15:3–4

We can know that God loves us because He gave us Jesus to forgive the sins of the world. (Story 30)

God loved the world in this way: He gave his one and only Son, so that everyone who believes in him will not perish but have eternal life.—John 3:16

We are only saved through faith in Jesus. (Story 31)

"Jesus is the stone rejected by you builders, which has become the cornerstone. There is salvation in no one else, for there is no other name under heaven given to people by which we must be saved."—Acts 4:11–12

As the Son of God, Jesus is both fully God and fully human. (Stories 32, 33)

Adopt the same attitude as that of Christ Jesus, who, existing in the form of God, did not consider equality with God as something to be exploited. Instead he emptied himself by assuming the form of a servant, taking on the likeness of humanity.—Philippians 2:5–7

Jesus taught about God and His kingdom. He taught that all Scripture is about Him. (Stories 34, 35)

Then beginning with Moses and all the Prophets, [Jesus] interpreted for them the things concerning himself in all the Scriptures.—Luke 24:27

People reject Jesus because everyone is born with a sin nature and wants to please themselves rather than obey God. (Story 36)

The Spirit is the one who gives life. The flesh doesn't help at all. The words that I have spoken to you are spirit and are life. But there are some among you who don't believe. —John 6:63–64

Jesus perfectly reveals God the Father and fulfills what the prophets spoke. (Story 37)

"Long ago God spoke to our ancestors by the prophets at different times and in different ways. In these last days, he has spoken to us by his Son, [Jesus]." —Hebrews 1:1–2

Jesus was the perfect sacrifice for sin, and He speaks to God the Father for us today. (Stories 38, 39)

He made the one who did not know sin to be sin for us, so that in him we might become the righteousness of God.—2 Corinthians 5:21

Jesus perfectly rules over the universe as the King of kings. (Stories 40, 41)

Everything was created by him, in heaven and on earth, the visible and the invisible, whether thrones or dominions or rulers or authorities—all things have been created through him and for him. He is before all things, and by him all things hold together.—Colossians 1:16–17

We can know that God wants us to know Him by the many ways He has revealed Himself to us, best of all through Jesus. (Story 42)

"The one who has seen me has seen the Father. How can you say, 'Show us the Father'? Don't you believe that I am in the Father and the Father is in me? The words I speak to you I do not speak on my own. The Father who lives in me does his works."—John 14:9–10

The Holy Spirit comforts us, shows us our sin, and guides us as we live for God's glory. (Stories 43, 44)

"The Counselor, the Holy Spirit, whom the Father will send in my name, will teach you all things and remind you of everything I have told you."—John 14:26

We tell others about Jesus so they will hear and believe the good news. (Story 45)

Faith comes from what is heard, and what is heard comes through the message about Christ.—Romans 10:17

Jesus became human to obey His Father's plan and rescue sinners. (Story 46)

"God did not send his Son into the world to condemn the world, but to save the world through him."—John 3:17

The church is all Christians everywhere who gather together in their communities to worship and serve God. (Story 47)

Every day they devoted themselves to meeting together in the temple, and broke bread from house to house. They ate their food with joyful and sincere hearts, praising God and enjoying the favor of all the people.—Acts 2:46–47

Anyone who trusts in Jesus can be forgiven of their sins and be right with God. (Story 48)

Everyone who calls on the name of the Lord will be saved.—Romans 10:13

Our mission is to make disciples of all nations by the power of the Holy Spirit. (Story 49)

"Go, therefore, and make disciples of all nations, baptizing them in the name of the Father and of the Son and of the Holy Spirit."—Matthew 28:19

We should praise Jesus for what He has done to provide our salvation and also because He is returning one day to make all things right. (Story 50)

"Worthy is the Lamb who was slaughtered to receive power and riches and wisdom and strength and honor and glory and blessing!"—Revelation 5:12

The church looks forward to Jesus' return when He will make all things new. (Stories 51, 52)

The one seated on the throne said, "Look, I am making everything new."—Revelation 21:5

Bibles for Kids

9781433644221
Hard cover

9781535922203
Galaxy cover

9781535922210
Rainbow Dust cover

*With many features
that bring the Bible to life!*

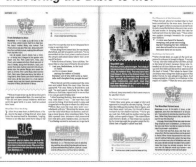

INCLUDES THE
FULL TEXT
OF THE

CSB

**CHRISTIAN
STANDARD
BIBLE**

Books for Kids of All Ages

AGES
0-4

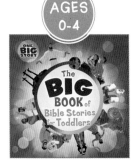

9781462774067

AGES
4-8

9781087715445

AGES
4-8

9781535947961

AGES
6-10

9781535934978

AGES
6-10

AGES
6-10

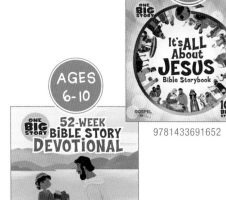

9781433691652

9781535946339

9781462796632